Step-by-Step Angular Routing

Learn to create client-side and Single Page Apps with Routing and Navigation

by

NISHU GOEL

bpb

FIRST EDITION 2019

ISBN: 978-93-88511-667

LIMITS OF LIABILITY AND DISCLAIMER OF WARRANTY

The information contained in this book is true to correct and the best of author's & publisher's knowledge. The author has made every effort to ensure the accuracy of these publications, but cannot be held responsible for any loss or damage arising from any information in this book.

Distributors:

BPB PUBLICATIONS
20, Ansari Road, Darya Ganj
New Delhi-110002
Ph: 23254990/23254991

DECCAN AGENCIES
4-3-329, Bank Street,
Hyderabad-500195
Ph: 24756967/24756400

MICRO MEDIA
Shop No. 5, Mahendra Chambers,
150 DN Rd. Next to Capital Cinema,
V.T. (C.S.T.) Station, MUMBAI-400 001
Ph: 22078296/22078297

BPB BOOK CENTRE
376 Old Lajpat Rai Market,
Delhi-110006
Ph: 23861747

Published by Manish Jain for BPB Publications, 20 Ansari Road, Darya Ganj, New Delhi-110002 and Printed by him at Repro India Ltd, Mumbai

About the Author

Nishu Goel is a software developer currently working with IBM in Bengaluru, India. She has completed her Bachelor studies in computer science as in 2018. She works on Angular and keeps learning on the go. She loves to write blog posts and talk around the basic concepts of Angular at conferences. She is also the author of "Angular for Beginners" course on Udemy. With her work to apply technology towards sustainable development goals (SDGs) by the United Nations living in the villages of Jharkhand, India for three months, she has been awarded by the Prime Minister of the UK.

Some of her hobbies are: Working for community development with a focus on selective SDGs, Speaking at conferences, exploring places.

With this book, she aims to share her learning and understanding of the concepts of Angular Routing with everyone.

You can tweet her at @DcoustaWilson and read her blog posts at https://nishugoel.wordpress.com/

This book is dedicated to
my Papa and Mumma for
supporting what I wish to
do at every step of my life.

Foreword

Routing is one of the most important concepts for Angular developers. Whether you are just getting started in web development, or are an Angular expert, the mapping between the URL bar and the state of your application is a critical piece of functionality. Routing bridges the gaps between the individually addressable page model of the past and the rich client-side single page applications of today.

The Angular router is very powerful and this comes with some complexity. In the early days of Angular, it took the Angular team a few tries to get all of the complexity right. Nishu's guide to the router covers everything that an Angular developer will need to know to take care of the most common use cases, but she also covers more advanced strategies that will take developers' skill sets to the next level.

By acting as a guide to each of the learning steps that Angular developers should take in their journey with the router, she accelerates the learning process and hits important markers along the road, such as the nuances of handling asynchronicity with the router.

With this book, Nishu cements her place as a rising star in the Angular community.

Stephen Fluin, Developer Relations Lead, Angular

Preface

Building web applications has been done using HTML, JavaScript in the past a lot. When it comes to building large applications, libraries like Dojo, knockout etc. were used at a large scale. In 2009, the web developer community was taken by a storm when AngularJS was introduced. Misko Hevery and Adam Abronsbuilt it as a side project at Google and since then, this framework is not stopping to amaze people and help them build applications much faster and efficiently.

With the constant upgrades to this framework, it is growing more and more user-friendly and is now called Angular after the first version which was called AngularJS. From Angular 2 to the current version of Angular, the widely used name is just Angular irrespective of the version number.

At the time of writing this book, the version of Angular used is 7.3.7 and is very soon to be upgraded to Angular 8.

Some of the amazing features of Angular framework make it a widely-used framework for building single-page web applications. And one of the things that attracted me the most towards Angular framework was the so-simplified routing and navigation techniques in it and how it is so compatible with the Angular CLI (command-line interface).

And this was one of the driving factors for me to invest my time into writing this book about Angular Routing, having gathered some knowledge about how Routing works in Angular. I thought it would be a good idea to put together whatever I have learnt about routing in one place. The book has been put together trying to simplify all the concepts required to understand Angular Routing and at the same time, making sure that the reader grabs the most out of it and is able to code along his reading through the book.

The structure of this book is kept simple starting from the introduction of some of the basic concepts of Angular to get started, followed by the introduction to Angular Routing, basic set-up, concepts like guarding the routes, using parameters to route to different views, using lazy loading to improve the performance of the application etcet era.

I have tried my best to keep the language very simple to understand and used no heavy terms, in the hope of making this book an easy read for the audience and also a good read for the beginners in Angular.

The major motivation for me to write this book came from the person who has lived Angular for years and is the one who got me started in learning Angular right after my under-graduate studies. Mr. Dhananjay Kumar a.k.a DJ is the organiser of the Angular conference of India, ng-India and is a Developer Evangelist at Infragistics. He is the author of the book Angular Essentials. He has always been an inspiration whether it is his knowledge, hard-work, or the passion to teach people and help them grow.

Another one of the driving factors for me was my interest to write a book on a technical topic and after having learned some concepts of Angular with my major focus on Angular routing and having a clarity about Routing concepts, I decided to go for it.

The major learning sources for me in my journey of getting my basic concepts clear were DJ of course, the Pluralsight courses by Deborah Kurata, Software Developer, Pluralsight Author, and the official documentation of Angular, angular.io.

This book has a GitHub repository associated with it and the link to the repository is shared inside, because as we all have heard, the best way to learn something is by doing it.

CODE ALONG!

GitHub Link to the working code examples for different topics in the book:

https://github.com/NishuGoel/AngularRoutingBook

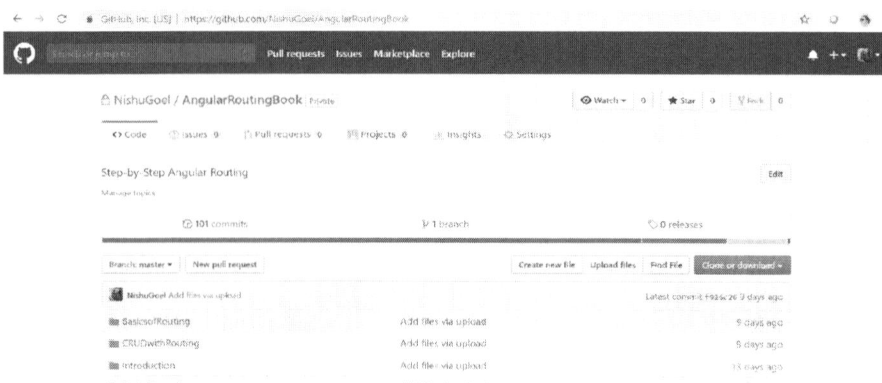

Errata

We take immense pride in our work at BPB Publications and follow best practices to ensure the accuracy of our content to provide with an indulging reading experience to our subscribers. Our readers are our mirrors, and we use their inputs to reflect and improve upon human errors if any, occurred during the publishing processes involved. To let us maintain the quality and help us reach out to any readers who might be having difficulties due to any unforeseen errors, please write to us at :

errata@bpbonline.com

Your support, suggestions and feedbacks are highly appreciated by the BPB Publications' Family.

Table of Contents

CHAPTER 1

Introduction to Angular

We will start this book with the introduction to some basic concepts of Angular. In this chapter, we will cover the introduction to Angular, prerequisites to start with this framework, the version history of Angular, and the important concepts to start building your client-side applications in Angular.

In this chapter, we will focus on all the concepts required to start your learning Angular routing and all the required starter files can be found in the GitHub repository mentioned at the beginning of this book.

If you are familiar with the basic concepts of Angular, this book will help you dive deeper into the routing concepts of Angular. However, if you are totally new to Angular, you can skill up your concepts around the following topics that will be discussed in this chapter, and then you are all good to go.

- What is Angular?
- Components
- Directives
- Services
- Modules
- Routing

What is Angular?

Angular is a JavaScript framework used to build client-side applications using HTML, CSS, and a programming language such as JavaScript. It is a collection of components which contain the code to execute the applications and have an associated template that displays the data on the browser. Angular provides features like binding the data from the code to appear on the template, expressive HTML, built-in packages to interact with different services, service for back-end integration, and more.

Angular comprises components, services, directives, modules, pipes, etc. to make our applications much more effective. There are so many applications built on Angular now and there has been a shift in the world of web development after the introduction of the Angular framework from AngularJS to Angular 7 (soon to be Angular 8). Angular started as a side project in 2009 by Misko Hevery and Adam Abrons to help build web applications using HTML tags. The name *Angular* comes from the angle brackets used for HTML tags.

The basic structure of Angular includes:

- NgModules
- Components
- Directives
- Services and Dependency Injection
- Routing
- Data binding

We will start by taking a look at how to set up a development environment for building applications with Angular.

Setting up a development environment

To build Angular applications, we would need to connect many dependencies, web development servers, and packages to each other. But to build and set up an Angular application from scratch takes some time.

Angular provides us with a command line tool for creating the Angular apps called Angular CLI.

Angular CLI provides us with all the required dependencies, boilerplates, takes care of the web pack configuration, unit test configuration, and transpiles TypeScript files to JavaScript.

To install Angular CLI on our local machine, we can use the node package manager npm.

Node.js can be downloaded from the browser at the following link as per your operating system:

https://nodejs.org/en/download/

Once it is installed, you can check to confirm if Node.js is installed properly in your machine.

To check if node is installed properly, use the following command:

node -version OR node -v

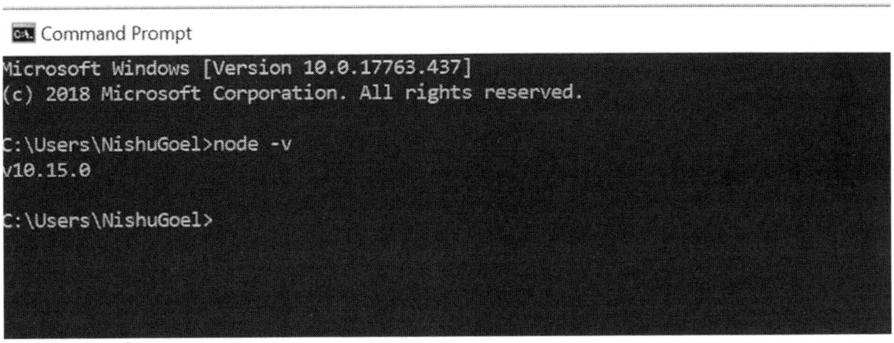

Fig 1.1

When we install node, it also installs the npm package manager along with itself. To check if npm is installed properly in your machine, use the following command as shown in the following screenshot:

npm -version OR npm -v

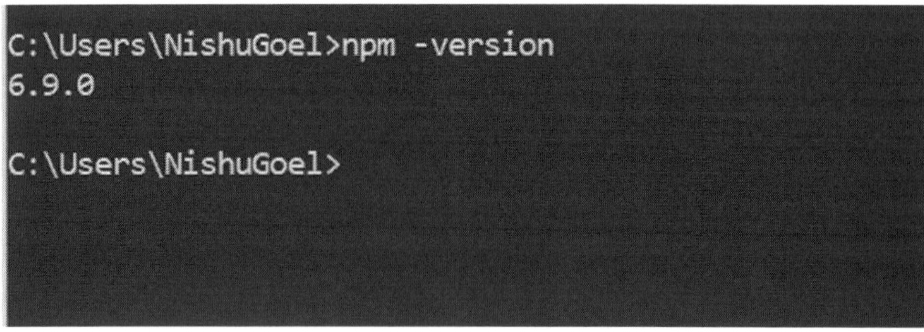

Fig 1.2

With node and npm installed, you can go ahead and install Angular CLI using the following command:

npm install -g @angular/cli

To check if Angular CLI is installed properly, use the command given below:

ng version OR ng v

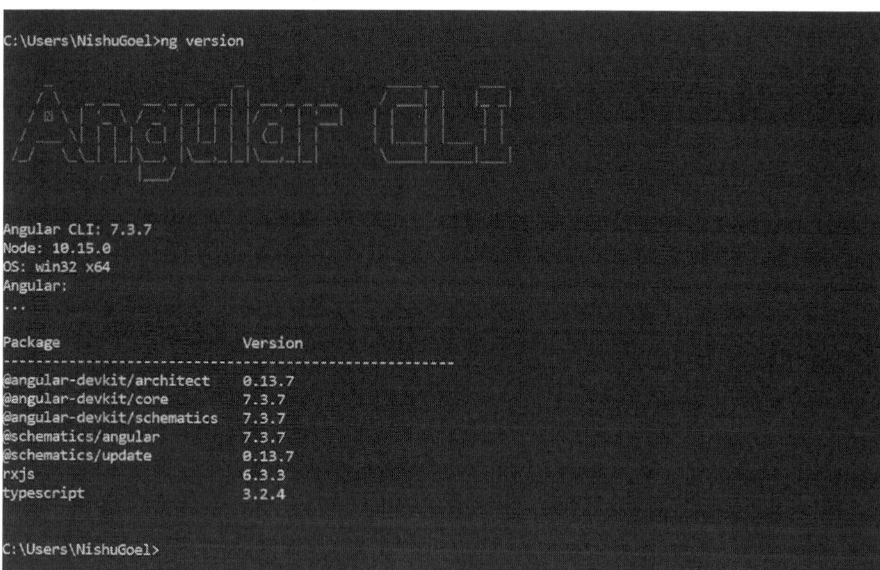

Fig 1.3

With Angular CLI installed, you are good to proceed further. Now, you can create an Angular project with the help of Angular CLI and CLI does the work for you such as injecting required services, getting boilerplates, and so on.

To create a new Angular Project with the help of CLI, use the following command:

ng new <project-name>

With the later versions of Angular, when you create a new project and before moving further, CLI asks if you want to add routing to your application and builds the project accordingly. We will discuss routing later in this chapter. CLI also asks the styling framework you would like to use. You can choose any as per your requirement. It will then start building your project, which is shown in the following screenshot:

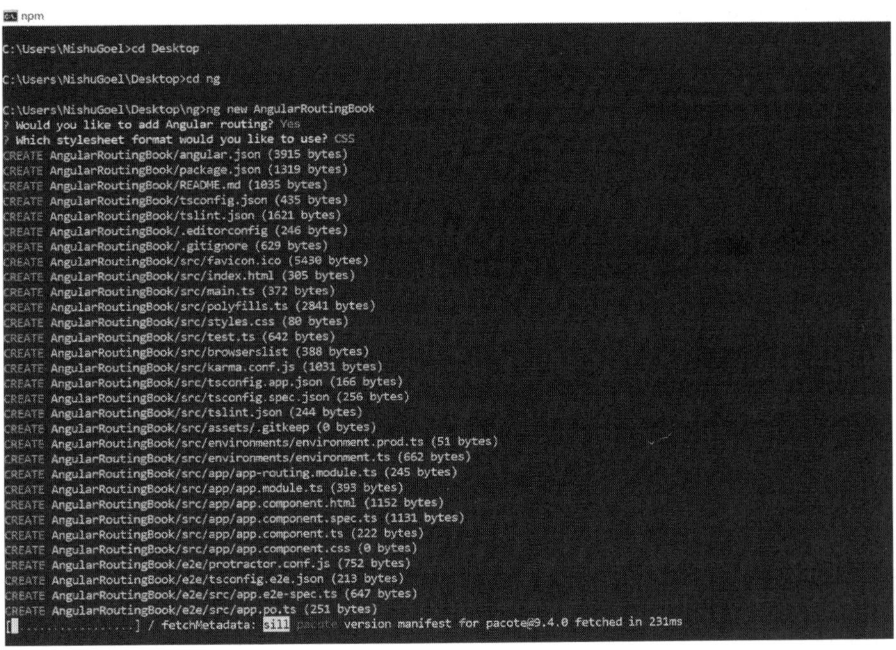

Fig 1.4

Once the project build is completed you will be able to view the following:

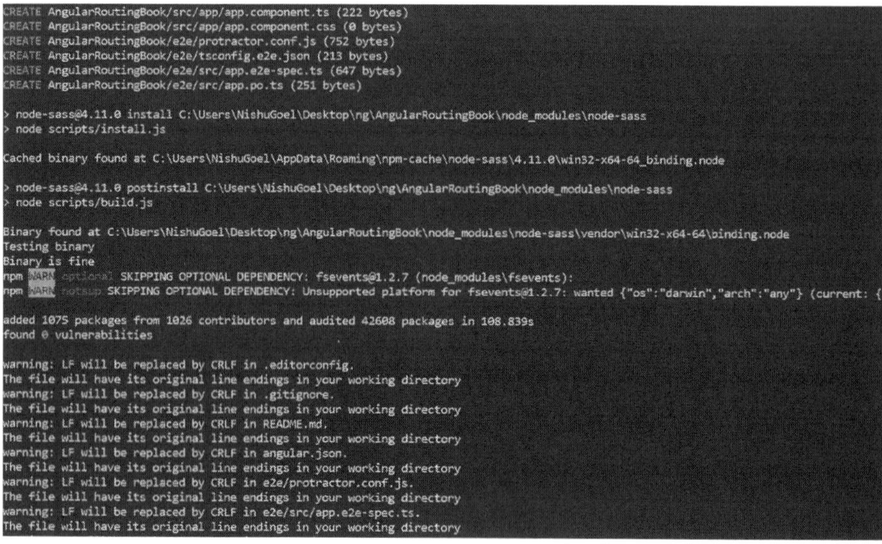

Fig 1.5

Once your application is created, you can open it inside your code editor. To open it inside Visual Studio Code, use the following command:

code .

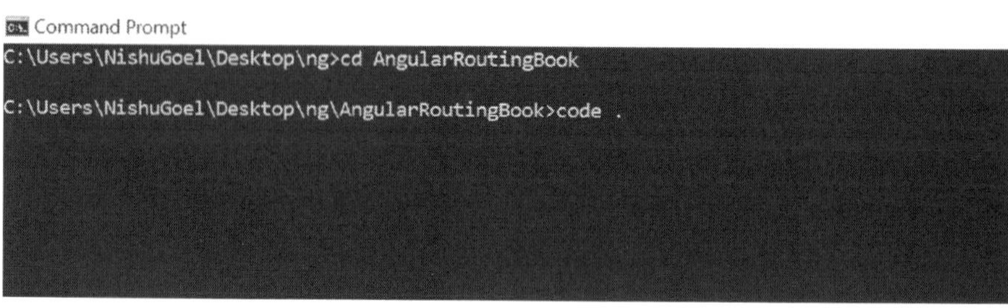

Fig 1.6

This will open the newly created project inside Visual Studio Code and the folder structure will look like this:

Fig 1.7

To compile your application now, use the following command:

ng serve

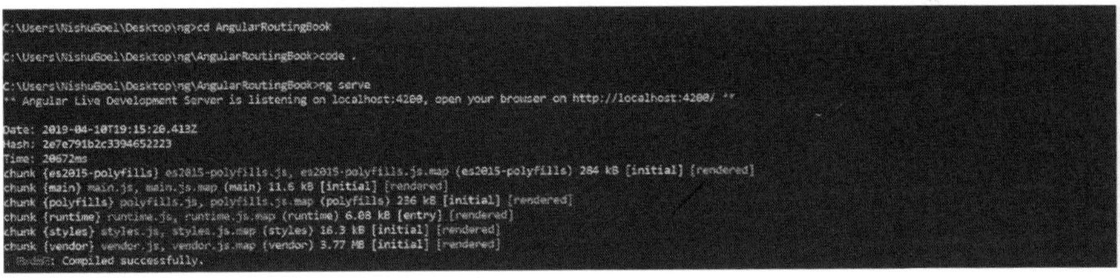

Fig 1.8

This will give you the introduction view of any Angular application with the title as the name of your project:

Fig 1.9

Component

In Angular, a component is the most basic building block which contains the code for implementing what should appear in the view. A component consists of a template, class, and a CSS file for styling your application.

A component is basically a class which is decorated by a `Component` decorator. This decorator makes the class behave as per the functionality of the component decorator. The component decorator contains the metadata for the class to behave in a certain manner.

Let us take a look at a `Component` class:

```
import { Component } from '@angular/core';

@Component({
  selector: 'app-root',
  templateUrl: './app.component.html',
  styleUrls: ['./app.component.css']
})
export class AppComponent {
  title = 'BasicsofRouting';
}
```

The `AppComponent` class contains the properties and methods for the implementation of our component view. It is decorated by the component decorator which contains the information for the class to behave as a component and the template which will appear on the browser. The import statement includes the important files that we need.

To create a component from the CLI, we use the following command:

ng generate component <component-name> OR ng g c <component-name>

A component also consists of an HTML file which decides what goes in the view. Every component has an associated template of its own.

This is how the structure of a component file looks like:

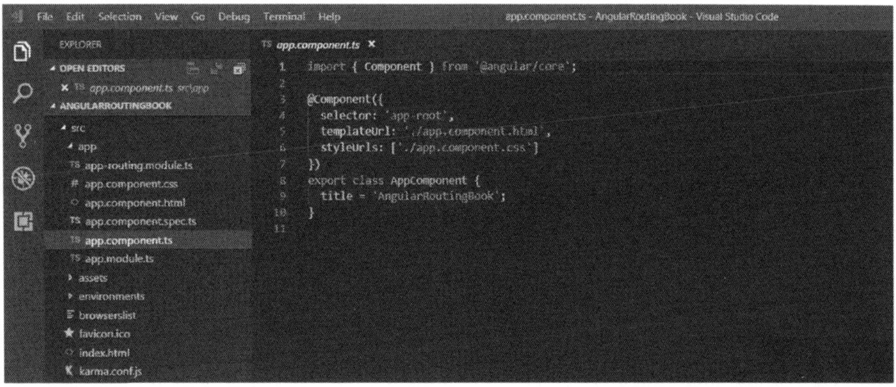

Fig 1.10

Directives

When we want to add a specified behavior to an element, we can use a directive. Directives change the structure of the **Document Object Model** (**DOM**), behaviors, and more. There are three types of directives in Angular, which are as follows:

- Components
- Attribute directives
- Structure directives

Components are also a type of directives which have a template associated with them. The attribute directives are used to change the appearance and behavior of the DOM, and the structure directives are used to change the layout of the DOM by adding or removing elements.

Similarly, the directives are used as class decorators using the `@Directive` decorator. We can also create custom attribute directives in Angular and use them to modify the DOM as per our requirements.

We can create a directive in Angular by using the following command:

```
ng generate directive <directive-name> OR ng g d <directive-name>
```

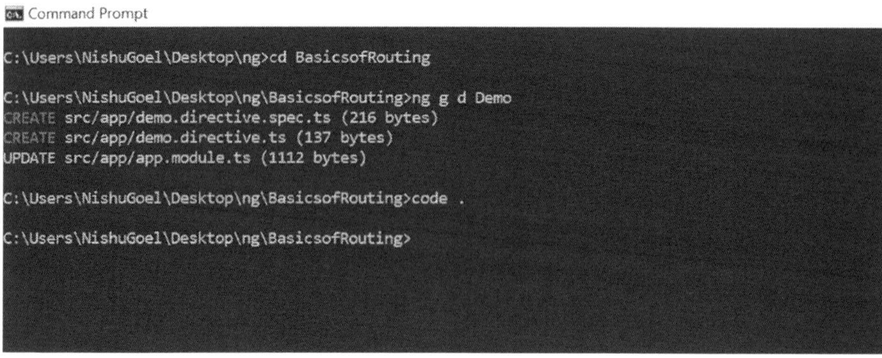

Fig 1.11

The structure of a directive in our Angular application looks like as shown in the following screenshot:

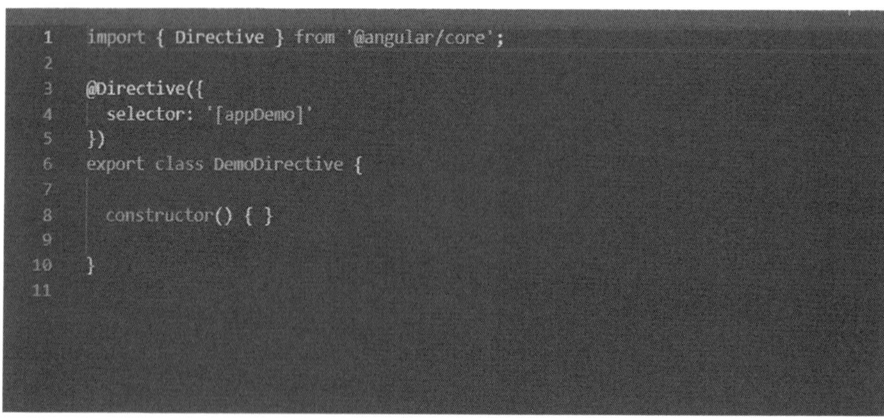

Fig 1.12

Services

When we have two or more components and we want to share data among them, we can use component communication techniques. Some of them use input, output, template ref. variable, and more. However, when we have components which do not share anything among themselves, services are used for their communication.

So basically, to implement any functionality that is independent of the component, we use services. Now, when you want to use this functionality inside your service for a particular component, you can inject this service inside that module.

To create a service from the CLI, we use the following command:

ng generate service <service-name> OR ng g s <service-name>

```
C:\Users\NishuGoel\Desktop\ng\BasicsofRouting>ng generate service Demo
CREATE src/app/demo.service.spec.ts (323 bytes)
CREATE src/app/demo.service.ts (133 bytes)

C:\Users\NishuGoel\Desktop\ng\BasicsofRouting>
```

Fig 1.13

The service file looks like this after creating it from the CLI:

```
import { Injectable } from '@angular/core';

@Injectable({
  providedIn: 'root'
})
export class DemoService {

  constructor() { }
}

```

Fig 1.14

After building the service, we register the service inside the module as follows:

```
  imports: [
    BrowserModule],
  providers: [DemoService],
  bootstrap: [AppComponent]
})
export class AppModule { }
```

Fig 1.15

To use this service inside any of the components, you can inject it inside the constructor of that component.

To inject the service, use the following command:

```
constructor (private demo: DemoService){}
```

Modules

Modules are the classes decorated by the `@NgModule` decorator which help us organize the piece of code better. Some of the examples of the modules are `BrowserModule`, `FormsModule`, and so on.

It declares every component, directive, and pipe inside the application. It bootstraps the component, defining from where the application begins. It also imports all the required modules inside the module to get their functionality working and exports the module which may be required for the working of some other modules. The Angular module also registers the services required to be injected inside the components as `providers`.

It consists of the following arrays:

- imports
- exports
- providers
- bootstrap
- declarations

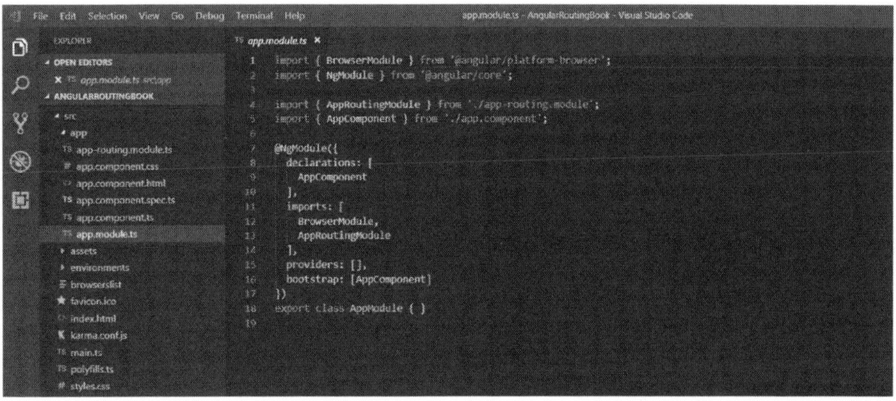

Fig 1.16

We can also create modules using the following command:

ng generate module <module-name> OR ng g m <module-name>

```
C:\Users\NishuGoel\Desktop\ng\BasicsofRouting>ng g m Demo
CREATE src/app/demo/demo.module.ts (188 bytes)

C:\Users\NishuGoel\Desktop\ng\BasicsofRouting>
```

Fig 1.17

In the following screenshot, this is how the newly created module looks like. It is decorated by the NgModule decorator which makes the class behave as a module:

```
import { NgModule } from '@angular/core';
import { CommonModule } from '@angular/common';

@NgModule({
  declarations: [],
  imports: [
    CommonModule
  ]
})
export class DemoModule { }
```

Fig 1.18

Routing

Angular applications are **single-page applications** (**SPAs**). When we need to change the view of the application from one view to another, we cannot really navigate to some other page within the application. Also, when we need to navigate from one view to another or you can say from one component to another component, we use routing. Routing helps us route from one view of the page to another view, providing different template views with different information.

To navigate from the view of one component to another component, we need to define route configurations.

We import `RouterModule` to perform routing and define the routes as follows:

```
import { NgModule } from '@angular/core';
import { Routes, RouterModule } from '@angular/router';
import { HomeComponent } from './home/home.component';
import { NextComponent } from './next/next.component';
import { PageNotFoundComponent } from './page-not-found/page-not-found.component';
import { ThirdComponent } from './third/third.component';
import { GetUserComponent } from './get-user/get-user.component';

const routes: Routes = [
  {path: 'home', component: HomeComponent},
  {path: 'third', component: ThirdComponent},
  {path: 'next', component: NextComponent, children: [
    {path: 'users', component: GetUserComponent}
  ]},
  {path: '', redirectTo: 'home', pathMatch: 'full'},
  {path: '**', component: PageNotFoundComponent}
];

@NgModule({
  imports: [RouterModule.forRoot(routes)],
  exports: [RouterModule]
})
export class AppRoutingModule { }
```

Fig 1.19

With the later versions of Angular, the CLI asks if we need routing for our application, and creates `AppRoutingModule` if we need routing in our application. This separate module for the route configurations helps organize the code better and exports `RouterModule` which is then imported inside AppModule. The AppRoutingModule module created by the CLI looks like this:

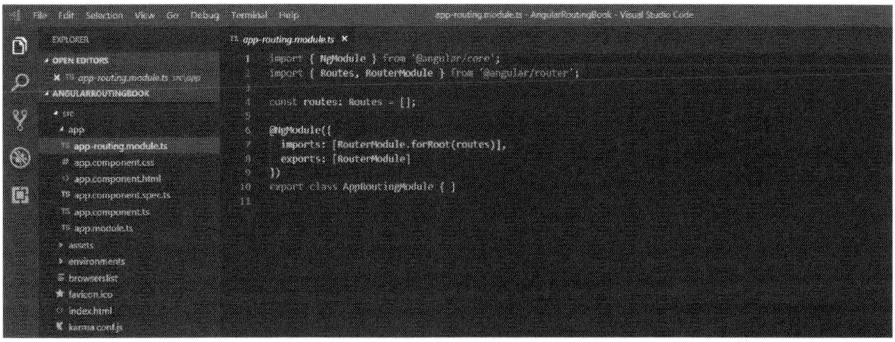

Fig 1.20

To use these routes, we can use the path value to navigate to any of the routes from a component view. We will see routing in detail in the upcoming chapters.

Summary

In this introductory chapter to Angular, we discussed all the basic concepts of Angular to get a rough idea of the structure and anatomy of Angular. The topics important to get started with Angular routing have been explained briefly. By the end of this chapter, the reader must be able to form a basic understanding of the core concepts of Angular such as components which are the basic building blocks of Angular, modules which contain and import all the required components, directives, pipes, and more, services which help us use the functionality for components that are not related to each other. We also saw how to create new components, directives, modules, and services using the Angular **command line interface** (**CLI**). A small introduction to Angular routing was also covered to get an idea of what Angular routing really means.

In the next chapter, we will learn about routing and its importance at a broader level.

CHAPTER 2

Introduction to Routing

With an idea of how the structure of files is in Angular applications, we can move ahead to learn about routing in Angular applications. In this chapter, you will learn about routing in detail, how it helps build **single-page applications** (**SPAs**), and what is the significance of routing in Angular applications. By the end of this chapter, you should be able to answer all the why's you have regarding the use of routing in the web applications built using the Angular framework.

In this chapter, we will cover the following topics:

- Defining routing
- Routing and SPAs

Defining routing

As discussed in the introduction chapter, we do have an idea by now about what routing helps us to do in an Angular application. When you need to change the template view from one to another, the browser URL gets changed and you will see a different view from the earlier one. The working of routing in Angular is based on the Angular router.

What is an Angular router?

The Angular router is the official library with JavaScript implementation for routing in the Angular-based web applications. It comes as a part of Angular core packaged as `@angular/router`.

The Angular router is the one behind all the functionalities that we perform in routing from one view to another in an Angular application. It activates all the components associated with a particular route configuration. It not only helps to view another component from one component without reloading the page, but also helps us redirect the URL to the desired component.

In the upcoming chapters, we will learn about routes resolvers, route guards, lazy loading the modules; all these functionalities are used as part of the @angular/router package.

Let us take a look at the working of an Angular router.

The very first and foremost task of an Angular router is to navigate to the configured routes for the components which are routable. So, the routes components are configured as the route configurations and these configurations are known as **router states**. Once these states are configured, the Angular router will render this set of components and bring the change in the browser URL. This will also require the router outlet to be present on the template as a placeholder for placing the template view on that page.

And this is why the first step when working with Angular routing is to import RouterModule inside your application. The next step is to configure the router states which form a tree of the router states. To do this, the routes are configured inside the routermodule.forRoot() method.

In the next chapter of setting up a routing application, you will see the different ways of using routermodule.forRoot().

At a given point in time, there is going to be one route which will be running and that is called the active route.

Whenever the routed path changes, it brings a change in the URL of the browser and the activated route also changes. In the upcoming chapters, you will also see how the order of paths in the route configuration or you can say route state tree, matters a lot. It follows the depth-first search algorithm and matches the first route path with the entire URL.

Once the configurations of the routes are covered, we can see how the Angular router navigates from one route to another. To understand this better, let us understand the router lifecycle first:

- Apply the redirects
- Match the router state URL
- Activate the guards
- Activate the resolvers
- Activate the final view on the template using router outlet

The following diagram shows the lifecycle of a router:

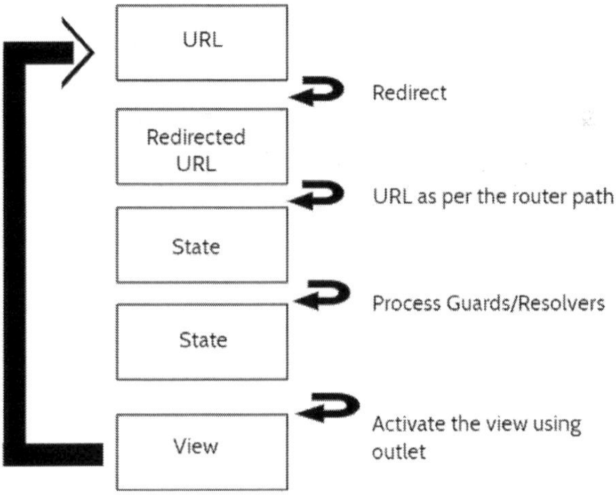

Fig 2.1

The router has a lot of events that take place during this whole process. The router events can be listened to using the router service with the help of an observable. Some of the router events are as follows:

- NavigationStart: When the navigation cycle of the router starts successfully.
- NavigationEnd: When the navigation cycle of the router ends successfully.
- NavigationCancel: This event is triggered when the navigation is canceled.
- NavigationError: When the navigation fails due to some unexpected error, this event is triggered.

- ResolveStart: This event is triggered when it is in the resolve phase of routing.
- ResolveEnd: This represents the end phase of routing.
- RouteConfigLoadEnd: When any of the lazy loaded route is loaded, this event is triggered to show that some route has been lazy loaded.
- RouteConfigLoadStart: This is triggered before lazy loading a route.
- GuardsCheckStart: This is triggered when the Guard phase of routing starts.
- GuardsCheckEnd: This is triggered when the Guard phase of routing ends.
- RoutesRecognized: As the name suggests, when the routes are recognized, this event is triggered.
- ChildActivationStart: When the resolve phase of routing ends, this event is triggered to show the start of the end of this resolve phase.
- ChildActivationEnd: When the resolve phase of routing ends, this event is triggered to show the start of the end of this resolve phase.
- ActivationStart: When the resolve phase of routing ends, this event is triggered to show the start of the end of this resolve phase.
- ActivationEnd: When the resolve phase of routing ends, this event is triggered to show the start of the end of this resolve phase.
- Scroll: This represents a scrolling event.

These events tell the state of the Angular router; for example, `NavigationStart` denotes the start of the navigation cycle successfully, `NavigationEnd` denotes the end of the navigation cycle, `NavigationCancel` is used when the guard does not allow the user the access to navigate to a route.

We can see a series of events from the browser by setting the `enableTracing` option to be true for the `RouterModule` object's `forRoot()` method or by injecting the router service and subscribing to the events observable:

```
constructor(private router: Router) {
  this.router.events.subscribe( (event: RouterEvent) => console.log(event))
}
```

Therefore, the Angular router makes it easy to configure the route configurations, that is, router states, and also helps to navigate to one route path to another with so many different router events running in the background which definitely can be looked at.

Routing and SPAs

We have evolved from the time when we used websites involving a number of HTML pages interlinked. However, it reduced to fewer and fewer and then what came to be used as single-page applications. SPAs can be implemented with smaller number of files whereas this will not be the same case with the interlinked HTML files. One advantage of using SPAs is that it does not need to download every page every time from the server. It just downloads the index.html and the rest happens on the client side.

If we inspect the main page of any of the websites based on SPAs, we will see that the first page to be downloaded is the `index.html` and there is no need to download all the pages one by one from the server.

You might be wondering that we load very little HTML from the server, with the data that is present at that time. What about the data that is added later. How does that get updated every time in a single-page application! To do this, the browser needs to change the data into HTML every time. That is a very logical question!

The answer to that can be obtained by comparing these applications to those traditional server-based applications. The rendering of data which used to be done on the server-side has a different approach with SPAs.

With SPAs, the data to HTML transformation is done on the client-side. Yes, you heard it right. The SPA-friendly browsers have something like a template engine running in them which makes the rendering part much faster and easier. Now, the data will not be needed to be loaded from the server every time.

The other question that arises is why do we need Angular for SPAs or do we need it at all?

The answer to this is No! We do not always need Angular to create SPAs but let us understand why Angular comes into picture then! When we are putting in a lot of data into one web page with the aim of creating a single-page application, the program becomes very complex and is not driven by HTML but JavaScript in that case. The code becomes very complex and then to handle such complex functions, Angular jumps in. Now we will not look at our application as a set of static pages with a lot of data in them; instead, we understand it as a complex program which needs to use all the tools required for a development project using a typed language like TypeScript.

Another very important thing to put light on, here, is that we do not need Angular to create an SPA because the website is an SPA but because the website is a complex program with a lot of code and complex functions in it. An easy-way of understanding this can be by saying that a non-SPA is actually nothing but a list of many SPAs. Many single-page applications comprise to form a single-page application.

Some of the advantages of using SPAs are as follows:

- Easier to deploy in production.
- Server to serve a minimum of three files—single page `index.html`, a CSS bundle, and a JS bundle.
- Faster page refreshes and no full page refreshes occur.

In the next chapter, we will see the setup of routing in an Angular application and how to configure routes, add guards, resolvers, perform lazy loading, and more.

However, the setup of a routing-based Angular application is done by the CLI. On the creation of a new project, it asks if you want to add routing to your application. If you say yes, the CLI creates and configures this separate routing module. However, if the developer is not sure whether to add routing or not, he can say No but can definitely add it manually later when required. On the CLI, it looks like this:

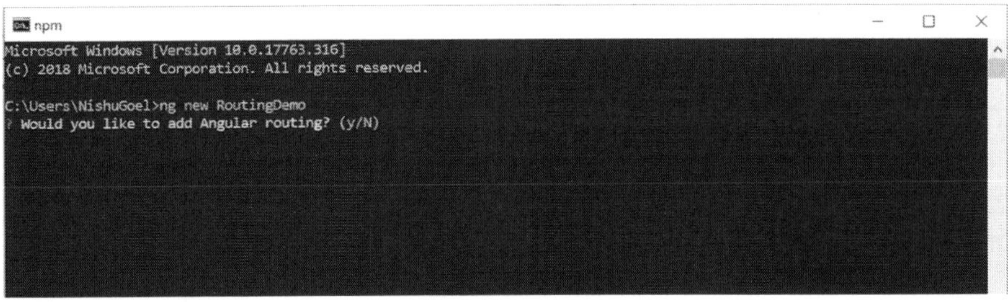

Fig 2.2

Summary

In this chapter, we saw what routing actually means and what role does it play in SPAs. We also learned about the lifecycle of Angular router and how it makes the task of implementing different views on the same page by simply changing the URLs much easier. Some of the advantages of SPAs were also covered in the chapter.

In the next chapter, we will start with setting up our routing-based Angular application. With the later versions of Angular, the CLI does almost all the tasks of setting up a routing-based Angular application for us. It simply asks if you need to add routing and if the answer is yes, it creates a separate routing module and exports `RouterModule` from this new routing module.

CHAPTER 3
Basics of Routing

In this chapter, you will learn about the basic concepts of routing. It will cover the topics from setting up an Angular routing application to the usage of different components and directives required to work with routing in Angular. By the end of this chapter, you will be able to create a very basic routing application which enables you to navigate from one view to another.

Some of the pre-requisites to start learning the concepts of routing are as follows:

- Good understanding of components and modules in Angular
- Basic understanding of directives and services
- Understanding of how components communicate with one another

In this chapter, we will cover the following topics:

- The basic setup of a routing application
- Configuring application routes
- Activating the routes
- Router outlet

If you think you are not too sure about the aforementioned topics, you may want to go back to the Introduction chapter and touch base with these concepts.

The basic setup of a routing application

As we know now, routing enables the user to navigate from one view to another as he performs different tasks on the **Document Object Model** (**DOM**).

Let us take the example of a simple website to understand the basic setup of a routing application.

The first thing we must do is go to the browser and type the **Uniform Resource Locator** (**URL**) of the website. What we will see then is the first view of the web application.

Now suppose if you click on some button on the website to look for the details of some item, let us say, you get access to some new information now which was earlier not available to you. Technically, the first view that you see when accessing the website through the URL does not have this information and this basically means that the data you receive on the click of the button may be contained in some other view, in this case, another component.

And this is why we navigate from one view to another. To achieve this activity of moving to and from different views, we use routing.

The browser identifies the first view through the URL which directs you to the first component template, and then using different routing techniques, the URL can be modified redirecting to another component associated with that particular path.

To start creating your Angular routing application, the first step is to go the index.html file and look for the <base> element under the head tag. This base path is appended to the path of the server. To work with routing and navigation, set this element as mentioned below:

```
<base href="/">
```

This is applicable if the application root for your Angular application is the app folder. This base path is used for development purpose. However, when the application is deployed for production, the base path needs to be changed. One way to do it is to manually go to the index.html file, and another better way is to use the CLI to do it for you by passing the name of the sub folder. The command to be used on the CLI for this is as follows:

ng-build –base-href /subfolder/

The next step after setting up your index.html file is to do the necessary imports before writing the code for navigation. The import statement required in the beginning is in the following code:

```
import { Routes, RouterModule } from '@angular/router';
```

The Angular Router is a library package that contains all the required services, configurations, and directives required for routing. Once you have imported the preceding statement in the app module, the next step is to configure routes inside your app. The different directives that RouterModule provides are as follows:

- routerLink
- routerLinkActive
- routerOutlet

We will talk about these in the following sections of this chapter.

With the latest versions of Angular, the CLI sets up routing in your Angular application when you are creating a new Angular application:

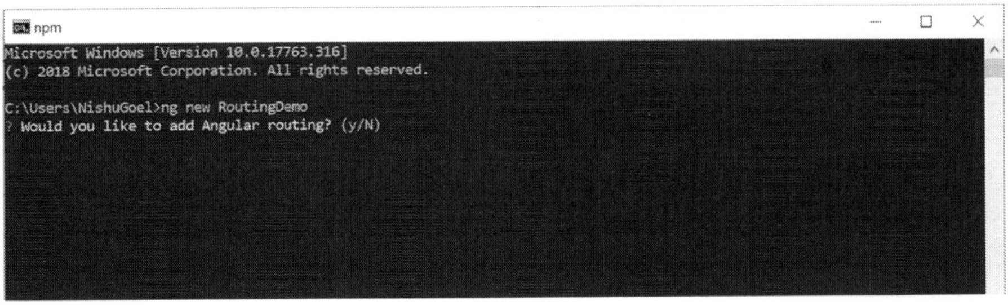

Fig 3.1

This will set up a routing-specific module inside the Angular application which consists of all the Angular routes configurations.

Once your application is set up inside the VS Code, your app-routing module is ready:

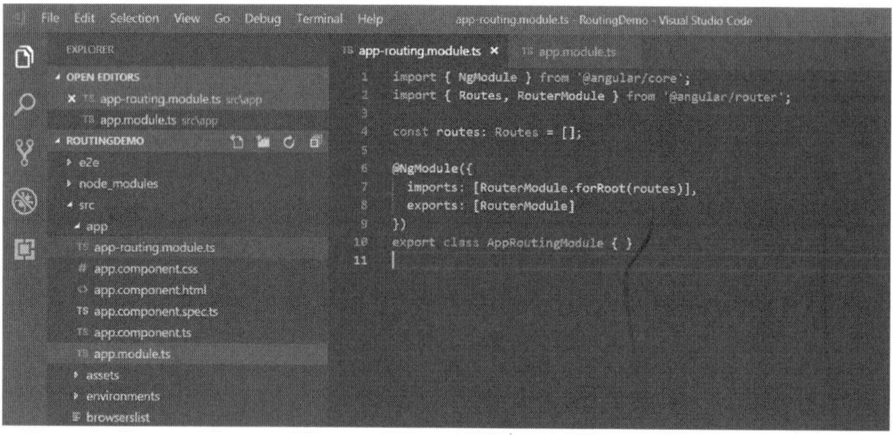

Fig 3.2

The CLI also updates the app module by importing AppRoutingModule in it:

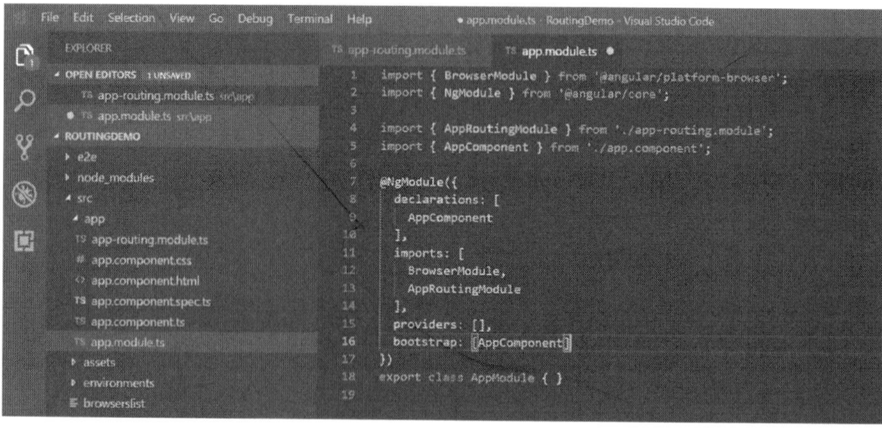

Fig 3.3

Now, let us briefly explain what the CLI has done to configure routing in our Angular application. It imported the Routes and RouterModule from the @angular/router package. It then imported the RouterModule inside the app module to configure the route paths and the components. It also exported the RouterModule to communicate with the app module through the app routing module.

Configuring application routes

To configure routes, there are two ways developers like to configure them.

One way is by putting in the route configuration inside the forRoot() method as follows:

```
@NgModule({
 imports: [RouterModule.forRoot([
  {path: 'home', component: HomeComponent},
  {path: 'next', component: NextComponent},
  {path: '', redirectTo: 'home'}
 ])],
 exports: [RouterModule]
})
```

The other way is by using a variable to refer to the array of routes and then configuring them separately.

```
const routes: Routes = [
 {path: 'home', component: HomeComponent},
 {path: 'next', component: NextComponent},
 {path: '', redirectTo: 'home'}
];
@NgModule({
 imports: [RouterModule.forRoot(routes)],
 exports: [RouterModule]
})
```

After you have configured these routes, let us try to understand the usage of path and component properties inside the route configuration.

To configure a route, you need to specify its path and the component view it should refer to. Let us say you want to navigate from your Home view to the Contact section. The information to be present on the Contact view is available in another component say, ContactComponent. Now to route to the ContactComponent view from your HomeComponent, you will use the following command:

```
{path: 'contact', Component: ContactComponent}
```

Now when the URL gets appended or modified by the contact path in it, it directs you to the ContactComponent view and shows that information.

To set up different routes for the component views, let us use some route configurations:

```
{path: 'home', component: HomeComponent},
{path: 'next', component: NextComponent},
{path: 'third', component: ThirdComponent},
{path: '', redirectTo: 'home', pathMatch: 'full'},
{path: '**', component: NotFoundComponent}
```

The first component to be displayed is the HomeComponent which is the primary outlet. The primary outlet is the first outlet that you have placed in the app component template. From the app component, the view is directed to the HomeComponent. In the next route, you need to specify a default route in case there are no route segments. This is done by using an empty path which will redirect you to the same Home page which is the primary view for your application. This default route has the pathMatch property which is matched to full when the entire path in the URL is empty.

In case, there is some path which we have not mentioned in the route configuration and Angular does not identify that, then in that case we redirect it to the page not found view inside NotFoundComponent. The asterisks refer to the wildcard route which is not directed to in our application.

Activating the Routes

To access the routes on the template, we use the routerLink directive to link it with the path to be displayed on the change of the view:

```
<a routerLink="/next"> Next</a>
<a routerLink="/third">Third</a>
```

Now, other than these two paths, if the user passes any other in the URL, it will get redirected to the NotFoundComponent component.

This is a short technique of using the routerLink directive. However, when there are arrays to obtain from the view you are directing to, you can also bind the routerLink directive inside square brackets and use it as follows:

```
<a [routerLink]=["/next"]> Next</a>
<a [routerLink]=["/third"]>Third</a>
```

With this, the routes are activated and with router-outlet placed inside the template, you can see the navigation working.

Router outlet

Router outlet is a directive used for placing the data on the template where ever it is present. This router outlet acts as a placeholder for putting in the Component data in the view:

```
<router-outlet></router-outlet>
```

The primary router outlet is placed in the app component template because that is the main template where all the data is placed. There can be multiple router outlets too; you will see more about multiple router outlets in the upcoming chapters.

Here is what it looks like now in the browser.

Go to the browser and type in the URL. The first thing is that it will be directed to the HomeComponent view as shown in the following screenshot:

Fig 3.4

To route to the **Next** component, click on **Next** and you will see this as shown in the following screenshot:

Fig 3.5

Similarly, the `ThirdComponent` object works as shown in the following screenshot:

Fig 3.6

In case we pass some new route to the URL which it does not recognize, it gives results as shown in the following screenshot:

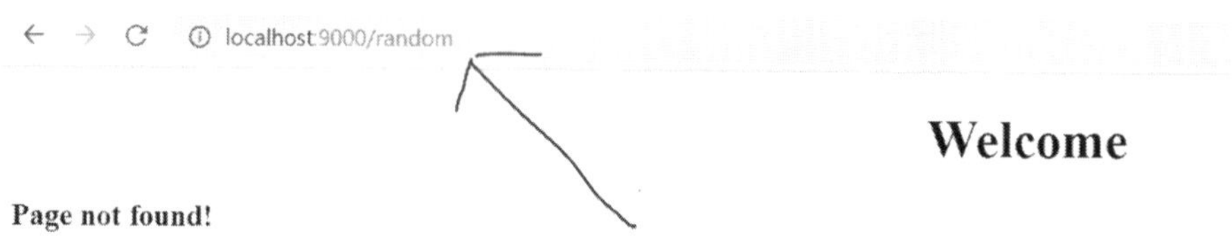

Fig 3.7

One of the important things to ensure is that when specifying the route configurations inside the routes array in the module, the order in which the routes are placed matters a lot. In case, you put `NotFoundComponent` above all the routes, no other route will be accessed and it will always be directed to page not found:

```
{path: '**', component: NotFoundComponent},
{path: 'home', component: HomeComponent},
{path: '', redirectTo: 'home', pathMatch: 'full'},
{path: 'next', component: NextComponent},
{path: 'third', component: ThirdComponent}
```

Fig 3.8

It shows Page not Found! for all the URL paths now. So, the order of placing the routes should be according to their appearance in the template.

Summary

In this chapter, you learned the basics of routing from setting up an Angular application to using routing to knowing the use of directives to place the view on the template. You learned how to import the router statements to start with the setup of your application and configured paths to different components. You also saw how to activate the routes on the template and finally place the view on the template using the Router Outlet.

CHAPTER 4

Routing to Features

In this chapter, you will learn about using routing by setting up different feature modules for the features in an Angular application. This will cover the topics of creating feature routes, accessing them, activating routing through the code, and essentially, the order of placing the route paths in a module.

Moving forward with the presumption that you have understood the basics of routing as discussed in the previous chapter and we will cover the following topics in this chapter:

- Defining a feature module
- Accessing the feature routes
- Activating the route through code
- Using `navigate()` and `navigateByUrl()`
- Order of route paths and modules

Defining a feature module

When you want to organize your code specific to the features and the functionalities that your app contains as it starts growing, feature modules are a savior. feature modules are used to organize your feature-specific code into a particular module. For example, if you want to put all the route paths related to the users in your application in one place, you can create `UserModule`, which is nothing but a feature module.

A feature module helps separate the code from the root module but is accessible everywhere throughout the application. feature modules collaborate with other modules and the root module through the use of services, directives, components, and so on.

To create a feature module, you will use the following command on the CLI:

ng generate module module-name

The structure of a feature module is like any other module in an Angular application. The next step is to import a common module which pulls in all the required common directives:

```
import {CommonModule} from '@angular/common';
```

You can also create a shared module and import it if you want to pull in all the common modules which need to be accessed by all the route paths.

To add routing to a feature module, you need to add an import statement to the RouterModule and add it to the declarations array. Since this is a feature module, you need to declare the Routes array by using forChild() in place of forRoot():

```
RouterModule.forChild([

 {path: 'next', component: NextComponent}

])
```

We will define the NgModule as shown in the following screenshot:

```
@NgModule({
  imports: [CommonModule, RouterModule.forChild( [

    {path: 'home', component: HomeComponent},
   {path: '', redirectTo: 'home', pathMatch: 'full'},
   {path: 'next', component: NextComponent},
   {path: 'third', component: ThirdComponent},
   {path: '**', component: NotFounfComponent}

  ])],
```

Fig 4.1

When naming the feature routes, it is a good practice to use the same name for the feature route and then add the other extended versions of it. This means that if you are creating a user feature module and if you want to access the user with a particular ID, you should be able to simply use user/:id where: id is a route parameter.

The concept of Route parameters will be covered in the next chapter.

```
localhost:4200/user

localhost:4200/user/:id                // Using same feature route path
                                       'user' throughout

localhost:4200/user/:id/edit
```

Fig 4.2

Activating the route through code

In the previous chapter, you saw how to use the routerLink directive to activate the route on the component template. However, one of the challenges you face when you want to use the code before performing routing.

To understand this in simple terms, when a user is signed in and you want to sign the user out using the sign out button before actually navigating to the home page, that is when you need to use the code before actually performing routing.

To achieve this, you need to use Angular's Router service. This service is injected inside the constructor of the component and using this, you can use the navigate method to link to the route path to navigate to:

```
import { Component } from '@angular/core';
import { Router } from '@angular/router';
@Component({
  selector: 'app-root',
  templateUrl: './app.component.html',
  styleUrls: ['./app.component.css']
```

```
})
export class AppComponent {
 title = 'RoutingDemo';
 constructor(private router: Router){}
 signOut(){
  this.router.navigate(['/next']);
 }
}
```

This navigates the user to NextComponent after he signs out of the account.

Using navigate() and navigateByUrl()

The navigateByUrl method displays the complete URL path, removing any other path present in it. This method is different from the navigate method when the secondary routes come into the picture.

Using the navigate method, the first route information will change but the secondary route will remain as it is and will not disappear from the current route.

For example, localhost:4200/next(secondaryroute). In this case, if can change the routes from next to third, that is, like this:

```
localhost:4200/third
```

Using the navigate method, you can change the route next to third, but the secondary route will remain as it is and this is how it will look like:

```
localhost:4200/third(secondaryroute)  //using navigate() method
```

However, if you want to replace the entire URL by the new route linked to, you can use the navigateByURL method which will route to thirdcomponent by replacing the entire route. This is how the code will look like:

```
localhost:4200/third  //using navigateByUrl() method
```

Let us see its implementation now. Inside LoginComponent, I am using the navigateByUrl() method to make sure that whenever the user routes from the Login component to any other, it will replace the URL entirely. This is how the code looks like:

```
export class LoginComponent implements OnInit {
 loginForm: FormGroup;
 constructor(private router: Router){}
 ngOnInit(){
  this.loginForm = new FormGroup({
   Name : new FormControl(),
    Email: new FormControl(),
    Password: new FormControl()
  })
 }
 submit(){
  this.router.navigateByUrl('/home');
 }
}
```

Let us see it in the browser now!

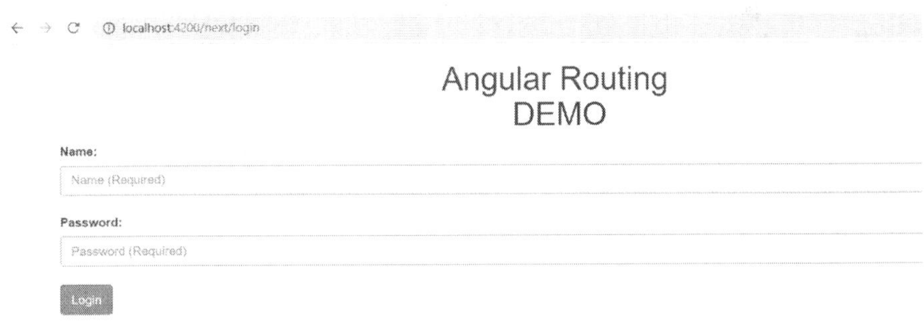

Fig 4.3

After clicking on the **Login** button, you will see the following screen:

Fig 4.4

Routes and their order inside the Appmodule

In an Angular application, the order in which you place your routes is of utmost importance as this order decides the routing of your components in the application. Let us try to understand this using an example. Currently, the appmodule looks like this:

```
routerModule.forRoot([
 {path: 'home', component: HomeComponent},
 {path: '', redirectTo: 'home', pathMatch: 'full'},
{path: '**', component: NotFoundComponent}
]),
UserModule,
DataModule
```

Now the order that is to be followed looks very simple here:

- Homecomponent
- ''
- **
- UserModule
- DataModule

But this is not the order in which an Angular application places its routes. Any routes which are explicitly defined in a module are always considered after the feature modules that are imported.

So, the correct order to be followed here should be as follows:

- UserModule
- DataModule
- HomeComponent
- ''
- **

Now, let us take a look at the scenario where you have a separate routing module to organize all your route configurations. In the previous chapter, you saw how the latest Angular CLI version asks you to create a separate routing module if the application involves routing.

The structure in this scenario looks like this (AppRoutingModule):

```
@NgModule({
imports: [
RouterModule.forRoot([
 {path: 'home', component: HomeComponent},
 {path: '', redirectTo: 'home', pathMatch: 'full'},
{path: '**', component: NotFoundComponent}
]),
],
exports: [RouterModule]
})
export class AppRoutingModule{}
```

The structure in this scenario looks like this (AppModule):

```
@NgModule({
 imports: [
  AppRoutingModule,
  UserModule,
  DataModule
 ],
})
declarations: [
```

```
  AppComponent,
  HomeComponent,
  NotFoundComponent
]
export class AppModule{}
```

Let us see now what exactly is happening here.

In the app-routing module, we moved all the explicit configurations for the route paths and exported the RouterModule so that it is accessible to the AppModule. Now inside the AppModule, we have imported the AppRoutingModule which contains the route configurations followed by the feature modules that we are using for different features.

But here comes a challenge!

When you import the AppRoutingModule as an external module inside the AppModule, the order of Routes remains as it is brought in and Angular does not go to the feature modules at first.

This will break the routes every time at the AppRoutingModule level only. This is because the configuration inside the AppRoutingModule contains the ** path and this will be routed to every time before being able to come to the feature modules.

Therefore, it is very important to make sure that when you have routing configurations in an external routing module, import it in the AppModule after all the feature module routes.

This order in the AppModule will then look like as shown in the following code:

```
@NgModule({
  imports: [
    UserModule,
    DataModule,
    AppRoutingModule //AppRoutingModule moved at the end of all other modules
  ],
})
```

```
declarations: [
 AppComponent,
 HomeComponent,
 NotFoundComponent
]
export class AppModule{}
```

Placing the routes in a separate routing module now behaves in the same way as it was when all the routes were in the AppModule.

Use of a separate module for routing configurations

When the application starts becoming huge and complex, keeping all the route configurations inside a dedicated routing module simplifies the task quite a lot and helps in better organization. You would not need to see all the route configurations every time you want to make any updates in the AppModule.

Summary

In this chapter, we learned about the use of feature modules and how routing becomes so simplified by using better ordering and organization of route paths in an Angular application. We also covered topics such as creating feature modules and accessing them using the feature route configurations. We also saw the use of navigate and navigateByUrl, followed by understanding the importance of adding routes in a particular order. We also discussed how to pass routing parameters to view specific component data. In the next chapter, we will learn about Routing parameters.

CHAPTER 5

Routing Parameters

In this chapter, you will learn about passing data to your routes to get specific views of your component. When you move from one component to the next component and you need to pass some data, you use route parameters. For example, if there is a list of products on your current component and you want to view one of the products from that list of products. To do this, you would need an identifier for that particular product and this identifier can be passed as a route parameter to be viewed on the next component.

You will learn about route parameters in detail but before that, you would need to have clear concepts about the following topics:

- Configuration, set up and activation of routes
- Understanding of feature routes

Now that you know how to set up routes, configure them, activate the routes both from the template and the code, and feature modules, you are good to go with passing parameters to the routes that you have set up.

In this chapter, we will cover the following topics:

- Defining route parameters
- Working with route parameters
- Reading route parameters
- Optional and query parameters

Defining route parameters

When we need to access a particular item out of all the items present in the list, we have a unique identifier for that. We pass that unique identifier as a route parameter to our route and display the view of the details of the item associated with that particular identifier. These are the variables passed within the routes whose value depends on the chosen product or item.

In the previous chapter, we were sort of acquainted with the use of route parameters. Our goal in this chapter is to actually understand what that means and how can we use route parameters in our application. I will use the same example from the previous chapter here:

```
localhost:4200/user

localhost:4200/user/:id               // Using same feature route path
                                      'user' throughout

localhost:4200/user/:id/edit
```

Fig 5.1

Here the common route is user which is a constant route whereas :id is a placeholder for the variable route which is dependent on which product is chosen. We can have multiple variable routes too in the application.

For example, localhost:4200/user/:id/products/:num.

To configure the route parameter, use the following code:

```
{path: 'user/:id', component: GetUserDetails}
```

```
const routes: Routes = [
  {path: 'home', component: HomeComponent},
  {path: 'next', component: NextComponent},
  {path: 'next/:id', component: GetUserComponent},
  {path: 'third', component: ThirdComponent},
  {path: '', redirectTo: 'home', pathMatch: 'full'},
  {path: '**', component: PageNotFoundComponent}
];

@NgModule({
  imports: [RouterModule.forRoot(routes)],
  exports: [RouterModule]
})
export class AppRoutingModule { }
```

Fig 5.2

You have already seen how to activate the routes in the previous chapter. To activate the routes which have route parameters passed in, this is the syntax that is followed (from the template):

```
<a [routerLink] = "['/user', user.id]">{{user.userName}}</a>
```

```
<a [routerLink] = "['/user', 0]">Create User</a>
```

As you can see, in the first line of code, the ID of the user is passed and this is redirecting the view to the user details with that ID. However, if the ID is passed as zero, it will redirect the view to create a new user since 0 is not associated with any user as yet.

Similarly, (from the Component):

```
his.router.navigate(['/user', this.user.id])
```

This will navigate to the view of the user with this id and will appear in the browser as shown in the following screenshot:

Fig 5.3

The view displays the URL against the user with ID 5. But we cannot really see the data, even though the URL appears to be correct. So, this happens because we have just configured the route parameters but are not actually reading them.

To populate the view with the data contained in a particular routed-to component, we need to read the route parameters.

After configuring and using a basic example of a route parameter, let us now proceed to see how we can read parameters.

Reading route parameters

Till now, we have configured the routes and we can see the change in the URL, but what about the data to be retrieved? To read the route parameters from the activated component, we use the ActivatedRoute service.

This service helps to read the route parameters and display the data corresponding to a particular route. To inject this service, use the following line of code:

```
constructor( private activateRoute: ActivatedRoute)
```

After having injected the service, we will use the snapshot option of this service which actually provides the initial state of this route. To access the route parameter, we use the paramMap.get() method and pass in the placeholder for the route parameter as the argument:

```
const id = this.activateRoute.snapshot.paramMap.get('id')
```

After receiving the initial value, we would want to change the view every time the value of the parameter changes. To subscribe to the change in the parameter value, the service provides this paramMap observable which will get notified every time there is some change in the router parameter value:

```
this.activateRoute.paramMap.subscribe(){
 parameters => {
  const id = parameters.get('id');
 }
}
```

Using the snapshot option of the ActivatedRoute service

To use the snapshot method, the first step that we need to perform is to import the service:

```
import {ActivatedRoute} from '@angular/router';
```

Having imported the service, let us inject it inside the constructor of the component. This is similar to what we saw earlier in this chapter:

```
constructor( private activateRoute: ActivatedRoute)
```

Now, since the snapshot option helps to get the initialized state of the route, we need to give it a thought as to where exactly to place this statement which reads the data. Now that is when the lifecycle hook ngOnInit() comes into play:

```
ngOnInit(){
  const id = this.activateRoute.snapshot.paramMap.get('id');
  this.getUser(id);
}
```

Having read the route parameters now, let us check if we can see the data in the browser:

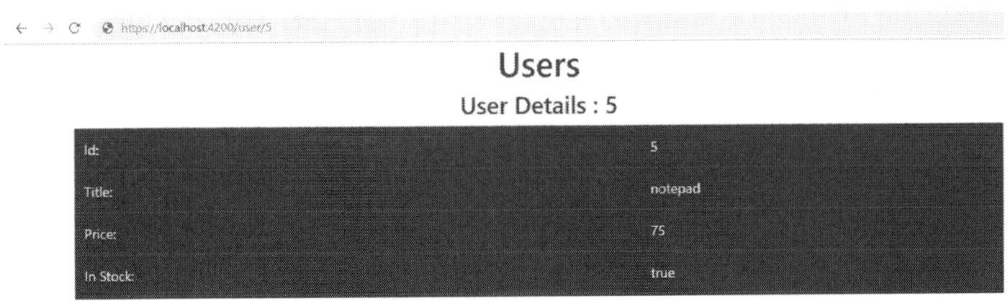

Fig 5.4

However, when there is some change in the route parameter value, the read route parameter option will not work. This is because the component will not reinitialize the data.

In such cases, when we need to capture the data for any change that has taken place, we need to use the observable provided by the ActivatedRoute service, that is, paramMap.

The paramMap observable will subscribe to the change that takes place in the value of the variable route parameter inside the constructor where we injected the dependency of the ActivatedRoute service.

After having imported the ActivatedRoute service from the Angular/ router and having injected the service inside the constructor, the paramMap observable will subscribe to the value of the change in the route parameter:

```
constructor (private activateRoute: ActivatedRoute){
 this.activateRoute.paramMap.subscribe(
  parameters => {
   console.log(parameters.get('id'));
  }
 );
}
```

Having looked at the usage of both the snapshot and observable, we need to figure out as to when to use the snapshot option and the observable provided by the service:

- Use snapshot when: You can use this option when you want to read the route parameters only once. You can also use this option when you want to keep the code simple and you know there is no scope for changes.
- Use Observable when: This parameter is expected to change repeatedly. You can use this option when you want to get notified of the changes in the route parameters and subscribe to that data.

After you have read the route parameters and are able to successfully view the data on the specific routes, the next bit to jump into is to see what the other optional parameters are:

```
@Component({
  selector: 'app-get-user',
  templateUrl: './get-user.component.html',
  styleUrls: ['./get-user.component.css']
})
export class GetUserComponent implements OnInit {
  user: UserFetch;
  displayData: boolean;

  constructor(private activateRoute: ActivatedRoute, private dataservice: DataService) {

  }

  ngOnInit() {
    const id= +this.activateRoute.snapshot.paramMap.get('id');
    this.getUser(id);
  }

  getUser(id: number) {
    this.dataservice.getUser(id).subscribe(data => {
      this.user = data;
      this.displayData=true;
    });
  }
}
```

Fig 5.5

This gives the output as shown in the following screenshot:

Fig 5.6

Now when you click on the **Go to this product** button, it takes you to the next route with the route parameter displayed in the URL:

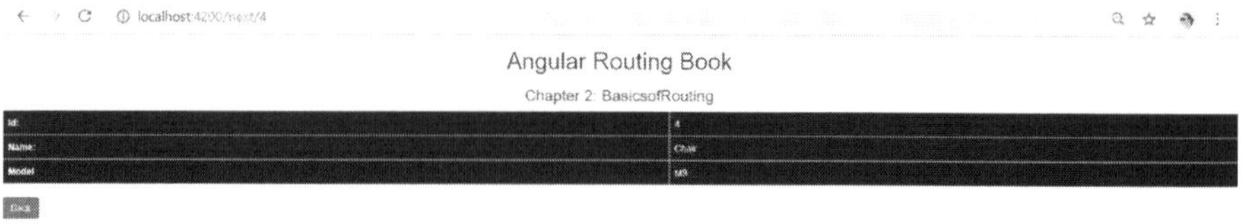

Fig 5.7

Query and optional parameters

When we want to pass in some optional information to the route, we use optional parameters. Option parameters make it easy to access the more complex information by having key-value pairs naming technical in the route.

To define the optional parameters, we use the `routerLink` array and pass them in using the key-value pairs:

```
<a [routerLink] = ['/users', {name: username, age: userAge}]>
```

Now since each parameter has a unique key, it is easily identifiable and does not complicate the route configuration.

The resulting URL then looks like this:

```
https://localhost:4200/users;name=Manish;age=42
```

As you can see in the generated URL, it has these key-value pairs with unique identifiers for each of the optional parameters so that no route collision issues will take place as such.

Reading the optional parameters

To read the optional parameters, we will simply import the `ActivatedRoute` service as discussed earlier and inject it inside the constructor. Having done this, we will put the optional parameters in the `routerLink` array and then finally use it inside the constructor using the snapshot option to get the parameters through the code.

We can do this using the following code:

```
console.log(this.activateRoute.snapshot.paramMap.get('name'));
```

Query parameters

When we want to pass the option information to the component but want to retain it at the same time after some operation has been performed on the component, query parameters come to be of great help. query parameters help to communicate across multiple routes, therefore, retaining the data retrieved on a particular component view.

The syntax that query parameters follow is that they start with a question mark and an ampersand as a separator:

```
https://localhost:4200/users/?nameby=this&age=some
```

To define the query parameters, we use the queryParams directive to bind the information and it is not passed as part of the routerLink array.

It basically looks like the following code:

```
<a [routerLink]= "/users", user.id [queryParams] ="{...}"></a>
```

From the following code, we define our queryParams:

```
this.router.navigate(['/users'].{
 queryParams: {...}
);
```

Query parameters also contain key-value pairs like the optional parameters. Now when we navigate back from the current page, we want the data to be retained. To retain the data, we can use the queryParamsHandling directive to preserve the data that has been changed:

```
<a [routerLink]= "['/users']",queryParamshandling="preserve"></a>
```

This retains the URL in the browser but we should not forget that we need to read the parameters.

Reading the query parameters

To read the query parameters, we will perform the same steps as discussed earlier. We will import the ActivatedRoute service from the Angular/route and inject it inside the constructor. Inside the constructor, we will simply use the get method to read the query parameters using the following code:

```
console.log(this.activateRoute.snapshot.queryParamMap.get(''));
```

This will finally read the parameter and display the data as per the query parameters.

Summary

In this chapter, we learned about the routing parameters which are used to pass a specific identifier to our route configuration. This is used to get the data corresponding to the item identified by the given route parameter. We also saw how using the route parameter brings in the change in the URL, but to display it in the view, we need to read the parameter using either the snapshot option or the observable provided by the ActivatedRoute service. Then, we learned about some other parameters like optional and query parameters.

In the next chapter, we will learn about child routes and how we can place and view one route within another route.

CHAPTER 6

Child Routes

Until now, we have very well understood the use of routing in an Angular application. We have also seen how to create feature routes to organize and implement our Angular app much better. This brings us to dive a little deeper into organizing the routes in a more hierarchical manner. This basically means that if we have some feature routes already created and we have some edit functionality to add to it, we will definitely need another component for this. A better approach would be to create this edit component inside the already created feature module. We can call it a nested route.

Before moving on to see the working of child routes, make sure that you are well-versed with feature routes and how they can be configured and routed to inside an application.

In this chapter, we will cover the following topics:

- Defining child routes
- Configuring child routes
- Activating these routes

Defining child routes

Child Routes help us organize our components better in an Angular application. We define a route hierarchy to organize and navigate to different components through Child Routes. Also, child routes make it easy to lazy load routes thus improving the performance of the application. Lazy loading is an important concept of routing and will be discussed in the upcoming chapters. These child routes are nested under any of the primary routes, which then act as the parent components having one or more children routes:

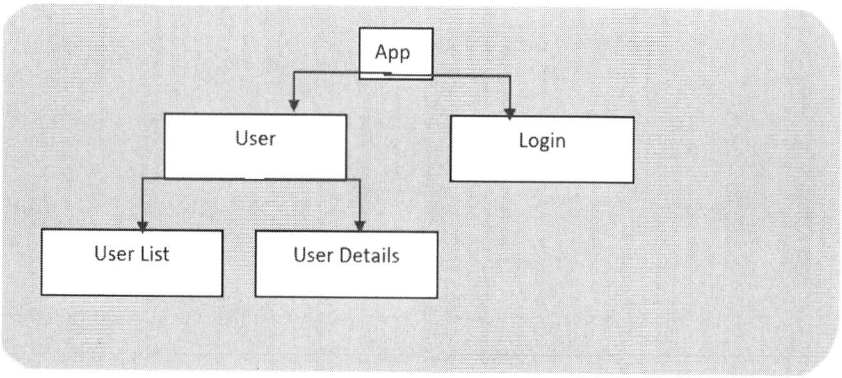

Fig 6.1

If we want to display a route component template, we simply put the router outlet element on the template and it appears in the view. However, if you want to display one route inside another route component template, we use Child routes. But the question still persists that how to display two templates in the same view.

To do this, the best approach is to use tabs to contain the different routes information and display whenever whichever tab is being clicked on. The result to be obtained on the click of a tab can be displayed inside a general containing component for the view. The first component for the view to be used as a container is shown in the following screenshot:

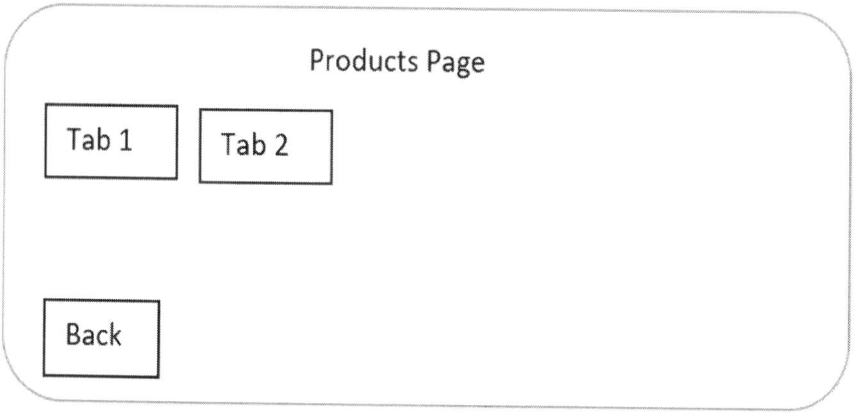

Fig 6.2

Tab 1 is one of the child components which will display its data when you click on **Tab 1** details. Similarly, **Tab 2** is another child component of its own and displays the results in the same view by displacing the first view.

Configuring child routes

To display the child routes, we place them inside the children array inside the route configuration. The code is as follows:

```
path: 'user', component: UserComponent, children: [
 {path: '', redirectTo: '', pathMatch: 'full'},
 {path: 'list', component: UserListComponent},
 {path: 'details, component: UserDetailsComponent}
]
```

Let us talk about what this means. This route instance is part of a routes array which consists of all the routes inside our application. Now for this particular route UserComponent, we need to create one or more child routes. To do this, we take an attribute inside this route instance called children. This child attribute is again a route array which will consist of all the child routes for this UserComponent. Now to match this route, Angular will display as user/<child> in the URL.

In this case, https://localhost:4200/user/list or else you can use https://localhost:4200/user/details.

Having configured these child routes inside the Routes array, we need to make sure that we declare them in the declarations array as well:

```
declarations: [
 UserListComponent,
 UserDetailsComponent
]
```

Another thing we can do is to display the first child route by default when the user goes to the UserComponent. This means that when the user tries to access localhost:4200/user, it will actually redirect him to the localhost:4200/user/list page. To do this, we can use the same configuration with a minor change in the code:

```
path: 'user', component: UserComponent, children: [
 {path: '', redirectTo: 'list', pathMatch: 'full'},
 {path: 'list', component: UserListComponent},
 {path: 'details, component: UserDetailsComponent}
]
```

Inside the redirectTo attribute of the child route instance, we use the route to UserListComponent so that the default page comes up to be that of the UserListComponent template. One of the most commonly made mistakes here is using a slash with the route in the redirectTo attribute. If we use a slash in the redirectTo property, it will actually redirect you to the Home page which is the role of the redirectTo property of your parent route instance.

In the code, this looks like as shown in the following screenshot:

```
@NgModule({
  imports: [RouterModule.forRoot([
    {path: 'home', component: HomeComponent},
    {path: 'next', component: NextComponent, children: [
      {path: '', redirectTo: 'third', pathMatch: 'full'},
      {path: 'third', component: ThirdComponent},
      {path: 'info', component: EditNextComponent}

    ]},

    {path: '', redirectTo: 'home', pathMatch: 'full'},
    {path: '**', component: PageNotFoundComponent},
  ])],
  exports: [RouterModule]
```

Fig 6.3

Now that we have configured the child routes, we need to place these routes inside the template to display them in the view.

To place the child routes on the template, we use the router outlet element. This element identifies the component template to be displayed without any name given to the router outlet. This is because it understands which route to display from the hierarchy. The user.component.html has the following code:

```
<div>
 <div>
  <a routerLink='list'>User List</a>
  <a routerLink = 'details'> User Details </a>
 </div>
 <router-outlet></router-outlet>
</div>
```

And how does the URL look like when we click on let us say, the **User List** tab:

https:localhost:4200/user/list

So, now we have created the child routes, but when we go and click on the child routes, they do not work for the obvious reason that we have only created the child routes but have not actually activated them. In the next section of this chapter, we will see how to activate the child routes that we have created and placed using the template.

Now there are two ways to activate the child routes. We can use the absolute path or the relative path.

The first view of the application will look like this:

Fig 6.4

Activating from the template

Using the absolute path:

<a [routerlink]= "['/user', 'list]" > User List </a>

Using the relative path:

<a [routerLink]= "['list']" > User List </a>

In the case of using an absolute path on the template, we put in all the required component route details inside the routerLink array. However, in the case of using a relative path from the template, we simply use the route name without using a slash. This will directly go straight to the list component from the current component which is UserComponent.

Now let us see how to activate using the code.

Activating from the code

Using the absolute path:

```
this.router.navigate(['/user','list']);
```

Using the relative path

```
this.router.navigate(['info], {relativeTo: this.route });
```

```
<div class="card"><div class="card-body">
<div class="wizard">
<a routerLink="third" >Tab 1 for ThirdComponent</a> 

<a routerLink="info" >Tab 2 for EditNextComponent</a></div></div></div>
<router-outlet></router-outlet>
```

Fig 6.5

We need to make sure that we do not use a slash while using a relative path because if we do, the relativeTo property will be meaningless then.

Fig 6.6

Summary

In this chapter, we learned how to use child routes in an Angular routing application. By child routes, we actually mean placing one route within another route and displaying it in the view. We learned how to configure child routes and place them on the template. We also saw how to activate the created child routes inside our application. We also learned the two ways to activate the child routes, both from the template and through the code using the absolute path or the relative path and the relativeTo attribute while activating through the code.

In the next chapter, we will learn the other type of routes which are called secondary routes. You can call them auxiliary routes too. They are basically displayed at the same time in the view and at the same level in the hierarchy of routes.

CHAPTER 7
Secondary Routes

In the previous chapter, we saw how one route can contain a child route in a view and be placed within a route. Basically, the routes within a route are called child routes and this helps us use many routes in a view just by containing it inside another route. We can also place multiple routes in a view without them actually having a child- parent relationship. All these multiple routes can be navigated to from one particular view and have independent navigation at the same time. In this chapter, we will see what secondary routes are and how we can implement multiple router outlets in a view using named router outlets.

The concepts around router outlet and child routes have been discussed previously in the chapters:

- What are secondary routes?
- Named router outlets
- Activating secondary routes

What are secondary routes?

When we have a component view where we want to display multiple router outlets with different navigation routes for each of them, secondary routes are used. Secondary routes are the multiple routes also known as peer or auxiliary routes.

To place the template of any route component in the view, we use the `<router-outlet> </router-outlet>` element. However, in case of multiple routes to be implemented in the same view, we would need to place multiple router outlets on the template. The first router outlet, therefore, is known as primary router-outlet. And the other router outlets are known as secondary router outlets.

A secondary route is just like another route which has its own child routes, route parameters, and secondary routes.

In a view, this scenario will look something like this:

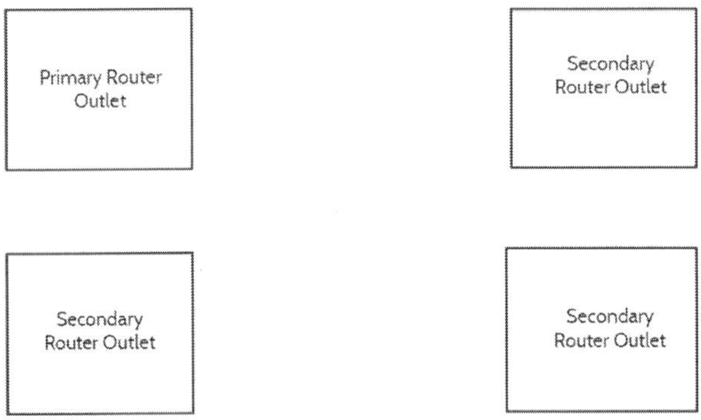

Fig 7.1

Let us take a look at one of the HTML files of an Angular project and you will see a router outlet tag placed in there to basically place the route component template on the view where router outlet is:

```
<div align = 'center' bg-color='blue'><h1>Dummy App </h1></div>

<router-outlet></router-outlet>
```

To place the primary route component template, we use the primary router outlet.

```
<router-outlet></router-outlet>
```

Similarly, to place a secondary router outlet in the same view, you will need to use the second router outlet which in this case will then be called the secondary outlet. We can place various secondary router outlets in the same view to refer to different navigation views and routes.

But the challenge here is how the Angular router would identify which router-outlet to use when. This means there is no identifier for a particular router outlet which tells the Angular router that this particular router outlet contains this particular template to be placed in the view.

And that is when the concept of named router outlets comes in. It is basically a concept to bring in an identifier for different router outlets so that the Angular Router knows which template should be placed in the place of which Router outlet.

Named router outlets

Defining a unique identifier for every router outlet that you have created in the view at the same level in the hierarchy of routes is what makes it possible for the Angular Router to identify where to place the route template.

When we say creating the routes on the same level of hierarchy, it means there is no child route created. All routes are the primary ones.

We can create a named router outlet (on the template) using the following code:

```
<div>
  <router-outlet ></router-outlet>
</div>
<div>
  <router-outlet name = "second"></router-outlet>
/div>
```

Now that we have placed the secondary router outlet on the template, we need to configure it in the code.

Setting up and configuring the secondary route

Creating a secondary route is very similar to creating a primary route path inside the RouterModule.forRoot array:

```
[RouterModule.forRoot([
  {path: 'login', component: LoginComponent, outlet: 'second'}
])
```

This outlet attribute is added as one more property to the route path to give the route a unique identifier. Whatever name is given to the outlet attribute that named router outlet is picked up. If inside a feature module, the route is configured inside the forChild() array.

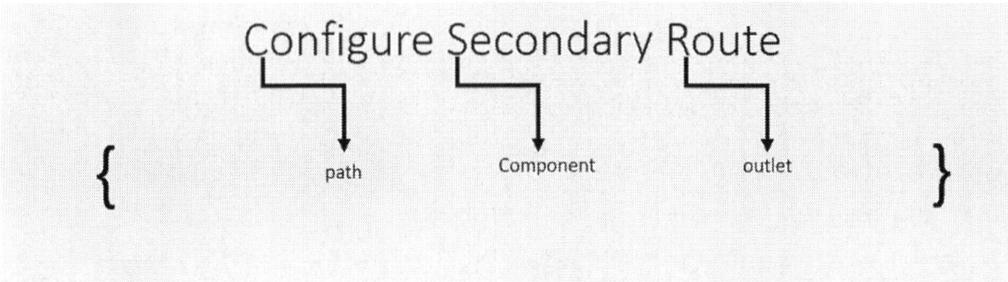

Fig 7.2

So far, there are two steps in the process that are done. Step one is to place the router outlet on the template wherever you need it, the second step is to configure this route inside the code inside the forRoot or forChild array of the RouterModule.

Let us see how the secondary route that we configured looks in the browser. Say, there is a route https://localhost:4200/User. You want to access the router outlet named second. It will appear in the browser as localhost:4200/User(second: login).

It follows the route path with the parenthesis to display the secondary route with the outlet name, colon, and the secondary route path. In the previous example, the route path is localhost:4200/User, outlet name is second, and the secondary route path is login

The next final step is to activate the route that we created.

Activating secondary outlets

Similar to the other routes' activation, in case of secondary outlets also, we activate the router outlet by placing it inside the template under the routerLink directive:

```
<a [routerLink] = "[{outlets: {second: ['login']}}]"> LOGIN </a>
```

The routerLink array contains the outlet property which is a key-value pair containing the name of the router outlet as the key and the value as the name of the secondary route path.

We can also route to multiple router outlets at once. We will first load the primary outlet and then give the key-value pair to the secondary outlet:

```
<a [routerLink] = "['/users', user.id, {outlets: {second: ['login']}}]">Login </a>
```

In the first part of the array, the primary router outlet gets loaded and then when the outlet's property gets activated, it loads the secondary outlet with the outlet name and the route path name.

This changes the URL and looks like this:

```
https://localhost:4200/users(second: login)
```

However, when you need to set some property when configuring the secondary route, you would need to write a code for that inside the component file and activate the secondary route from the code itself. To do this, let us see how to activate the secondary route from the code in the component class.

Activating from the code

To activate the secondary route from the code instead of the template, we use the navigate method:

```
this.router.navigate([{outlets: {second: ['login']}}]);
```

Similarly, to activate the route from the code but activate multiple routes at once, we will use the code given below:

```
this.router.navigate(['/users', user.id, {outlets: {second: ['login']}}]);
```

We can also activate the primary and the secondary outlet both at the same time. The name that needs to be given to our secondary outlets is chosen by us; however, the name given to the primary outlet is by default called primary.

We can also use the navigatebyUrl method as discussed in the previous chapters. This can be done by manually writing in the URL which you want.

```
this.router.navigatebyUrl(['/users/2(second: login)'])
```

This will help access the property at the same time when configuring the service and activating the secondary outlet.

When you want to clear out any secondary outlet that you created, you can simply initialize the outlet property to null.

```
this.router.navigate([{outlets: {second: null }}]);
```

The following line of code is from the template under the routerLink directive:

```
<a [routerLink] = "[{outlets: {second: null }}]">
```

This clears the activation of the secondary route and the primary router outlet still works unaffected.

Summary

In this chapter, we learned how to create secondary routes, how and why is it important to create secondary routes. We also saw the use of Named router outlets to identify uniquely the different secondary router outlets. Activation of the router outlet from the template as well as the code was also explained. The primary router uses the other outlet, gets it named by default and the secondary ones have the outlet name given by us.

In the next chapter, we will see how we can limit the access of all the routes to particular users by the use of route guards. As the name suggests, route guards will guard the access to the route for authorization, monitoring, and security purposes.

CHAPTER 8

Route Guards

We have been learning about navigating from one route to another by going to different component views. We also learned the use of child routes, feature routes and using different kinds of route parameters to provide specific information to the route URLs. We will now dive a little deeper and take a look at securing the route navigation. The name of this chapter has a literal meaning of that. When the user wants to route from one view to another, but let us assumes he is not a registered user and we do not want some information to be visible to this unregistered user, so in that case, the best approach to use is using route guards.

Before getting into the working of route guards, perform a quick check to see if the concept of routing from one view to another is clear enough for you to proceed. From here, a good understanding of routes, configuring routes, feature routes, child routes, and route params is a must.

In this chapter, we will cover the following topics:

- Defining route guards
- Creating a route guard
- CanActivate and CanActivateChild
- CanDeactivate

Defining route guards

In Angular routing, the user navigates from one view to the others using routes. These route paths are configured inside the routing modules and make it accessible to the user to access one route from another as per the code. However, in real-case scenarios, we have so many requirements where we would not want one user to be able to access all the possible route paths inside our application. One such example was mentioned at the beginning of this chapter. Let us take one more example.

Suppose the user is filling out a long application form and midway he wants to check some details regarding the form, so wants to go back to the intro information of this application form; however, if he does that, he will lose the details that he has already entered in the form. In this case, the application needs to put a guard where it informs the user who wants to go back that you will lose all the information entered on this page if you navigate back to another view. "Are you sure you want to leave the page?" Sounds very familiar! Doesn't it?

This is one good example to understand the use cases of route guards. route guards not only help us secure the application, but are also useful to monitor, authorize or prevent the user from leaving the route:

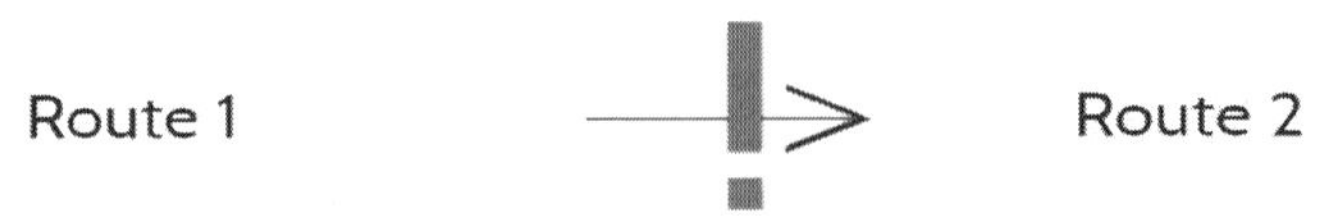

Fig 8.1

As discussed, the navigation from **Route 1** to **Route 2** would not just happen without any criteria to check. It passes through a route guard and then navigates to the next route. And this only happens if the route guard conditions are met:

Fig 8.2

The different route guards provided by Angular are all used for several purposes like monitoring, securing, and so on. Let us take a look at some of those:

- canActivate
- canActivateChild
- canDeactivate
- canLoad
- resolve

The canActivate route guard is used to guard the navigation to a route whereas the canActivateChild route guard will secure the navigation from one route to a child route. The canDeactivate route guard, on the other hand, will guard the navigation away from the route that is preventing the user from leaving a route. These three are the most commonly used route guards. However, there are two more types of route guards that are used for routing purposes.

The canLoad guard is used when the user wants to lazy load routes. That means this guard comes very handy when preventing asynchronous routing and is used in the lazy loading technique. This guard is used in place of the canActivate guard when using lazy loading to load the modules and actually loads the next module only if the guard gives access to it.

The resolve route guard is another type of guard, which as the name suggests, is used when you want to resolve something before anything appears in the view. We will learn about route resolvers in the upcoming chapter. When the user needs to prefetch some data before actually loading the next route component template view, the resolve route guard is used.

Let us now take a look at the order of execution of these route guards in an Angular application. The implementation of these route guards in a particular order is very important because, at every step, the user must be able to access the route with a secure and monitored route activity.

The order goes as follows:

canDeactivate
canLoad
canActivateChild
canActivate
resolve

Fig 8.3

Let us see why. The first route guard to be activated is the canDeactivate route guard. This will determine if the user would be able to leave the current route or not. The next route guard to be activated is the canLoad route guard. This guard checks if some feature module has been loaded asynchronously. Then, comes the third type of route guard which is checked when navigating to any of the child routes and then comes the canActivate route guard which is checked by the router if the user is trying to navigate to any of the routes. Then finally, the router uses the resolve router guard, which is meaningful enough, because the router wants to load all the data on any particular view only after it has checked all the other route guards. There is no sense of loading the data if the user does not get through the other routes.

Creating a route guard

A route guard is created as a service inside an Angular application. This means that this new service will be exported as a class and will be decorated by the Injectable decorator. Now that this service needs to behave as a guard, we need to implement this interface for it to behave as a particular guard. Also, this interface must be imported from the corresponding router package. We can also create a guard using the CLI with the following command:

```
ng generate guard <guard-name> or ng g g <guard-name>
//Creating the service for route guard
export {Injectable} from '@angular/core';
export {CanActivate} from '@angular/router';
@Injectable({
 providedIn: 'root';
})
export class guardService implements CanActivate{
 canActivate(){
 ...
 }
}
```

After implementing the interface, CanActivate in this example, we need to ensure to implement the method associated with the interface.

Now, the next step is to add the guard to a particular route:

```
{path: 'user', Component: UserComponent, canActivate: [ guardService
] }
```

We can share the guards also which means a guard can be applied to various child routes or to a parent route so that all its children are able to use this route.

canActivate Guard

The CanActivate route guard is used when the route has to be activated after checking for some conditions. This guard is mainly used to check if the user has already logged in or not. It is also used to give access to only some users for some confidential data.

Let us create one in the application now. When we use the CLI to create the route guard for us using the command discussed earlier. The CLI will implement the canActivate route guard by default, implementing the required methods inside it.

This is how your route guard looks like when you create it from the CLI before making any change in the code yourself:

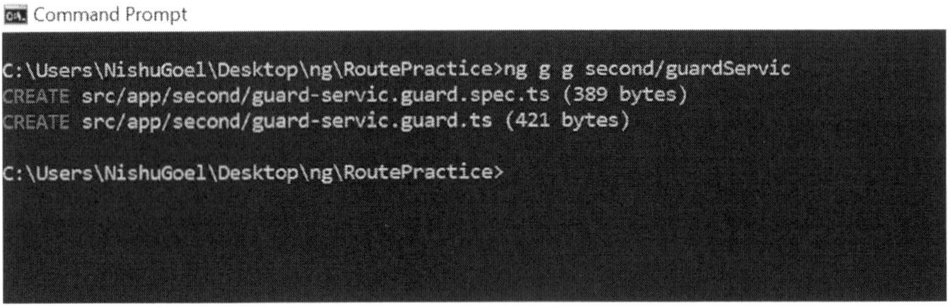

Fig 8.4

Inside the code, it looks like this:

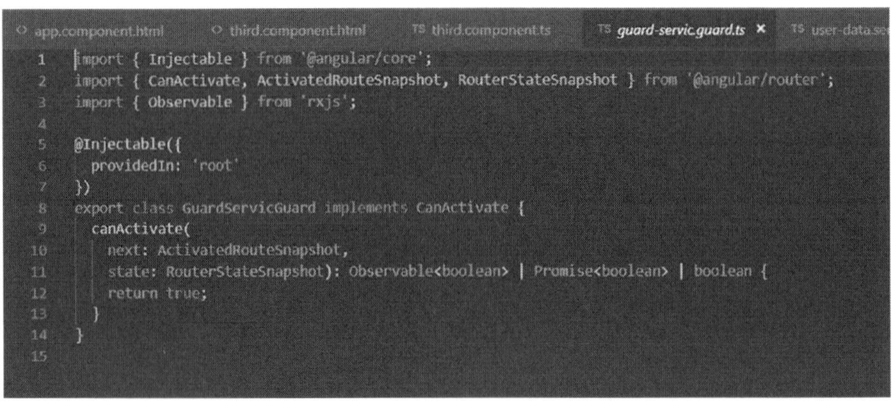

Fig 8.5

Inside the canActivate method, you can implement the functionality to check the required information before letting him continue. You can apply the canActivate guard then to all the route paths where ever you require it:

```
const routes: Routes = [
  {path: 'second', canActivate: [GuardServicGuard], component: SecondComponent},
  {path: '', redirectTo: 'second', pathMatch: 'full'},
  {path: 'third', component: ThirdComponent },
  {path: 'productedit', component: ProductEditComponent }

];
```

Fig 8.6

canActivateChild Guard

The canActivateChild guard is similar to the canActivate guard. When a child of any route is activated, that is when this route guard is called. It checks all the required information before activating a child route. The common usages of the canActivateChild guard are similar to that of the canActivate route guard. It also checks if the user is logged in or registered before activating the child routes. It also limits access to these child routes.

However, if there are some changes in the child route, the canActivate guard does not execute it again.

The working of a canActivateChild route guard is the same as that of a canActivate route guard.

canDeactivate guard

As we saw earlier, the canDeactivate guard is used when the user routes away from a route path. This route guard is used when the user is filling in some form and is midway through the form having some changes that are not saved yet. This is also used to confirm before leaving a route just to make sure; for example, the back button has not been clicked on by accident.

This guard is called every time the route changes from one path to another. One very important thing to make a note of is that this guard will not work if the user opens a different website or closes the browser.

Creating the Deactivate route

When creating a guard service, it will implement the canActivate guard by default as we saw in the earlier examples. However, we can use this guard in case the user routes away from this path. So here, we would need to use the canDeactivate route.

To use the canDeactivate route, we need to specify the generic parameter wherein we pass the component in which we have to use this particular guard.

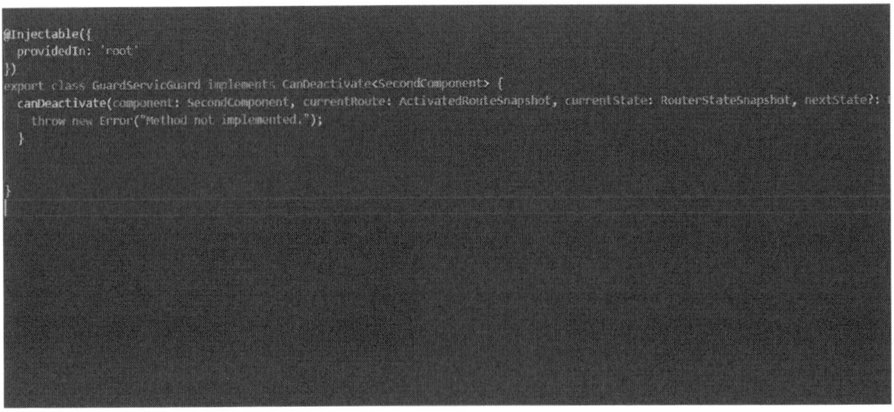

Fig 8.7

As you can see in the preceding code the first thing that gets implemented is the same component that we have implemented in the interface in the export statement.

The different values it can return can be either true or false. True here would mean to continue to the next route from the current route and false would mean to cancel the navigation process and be on the current route.

It can also return a Promise or an observable if it is relying on some other process and is waiting for the completion of that activity. Once it is complete, the navigation from the current route to the state route will take place.

The next and the final step after implementing the functionality inside your canDeactivate guard is to associate it with the component it is required with:

```
import {ThirdComponent} from './third/third.component';
import { ProductEditComponent } from './product-edit/product-edit.component';
import { GuardServicGuard } from './second/guard-servic.guard';


const routes: Routes = [
  {path: 'second', canDeactivate: [GuardServicGuard], component: SecondComponent},
  {path: '', redirectTo: 'second', pathMatch: 'full'},
  {path: 'third', component: ThirdComponent },
  {path: 'productedit', component: ProductEditComponent }

];

@NgModule({
  imports: [RouterModule.forRoot(routes)],
  exports: [RouterModule]
})
export class AppRoutingModule { }
```

Fig 8.8

Finally, you should be able to see an alert confirmation box asking you to confirm before you leave:

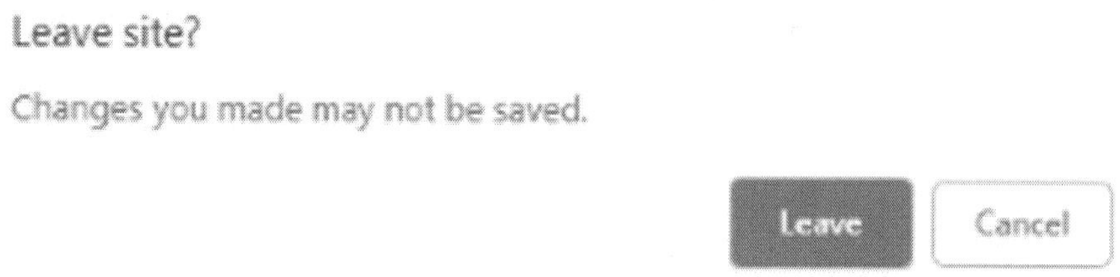

Fig 8.9

Summary

In this chapter, we learned some advanced and manicured concepts of Angular routing, using the route guards to limit access of the user to a particular route, or confirming before he leaves a route. We saw the different types of route guards available in the Angular/router package. We also saw how to create different guards with the help of CLI.

With a good understanding of route guards, we are all set to see more of the types of routes and in the next chapter, we will learn about component-less and grouping routes.

CHAPTER 9

Grouping and Component-less Routes

You might be wondering how many types of routes are there in all in Angular routing. We discussed primary routes, routing to features, and child and secondary routes. But then suppose you come across a route configuration which looks something like this:

```
{path: 'next', children:[
 {path: '', component: NextComponent},
 {path: 'login', component: LoginComponent}
]},
```

Probably, the first thing that would come to anybody's mind would be that the programmer forgot to write the component property here. However, that is not true in this case. In this chapter, we will discuss what such a configuration means and why do we configure it and group the routes in a route without a component property, that is, component-less route in detail.

In this chapter, we will cover the following topics:

- Grouping the routes
- What are component-less routes?
- Why component-less routes?

Grouping the routes

We have been working with a lot of routes in our application by now. We have also put our routes as children of one of the parent routes. So we understand what grouping is and how it helps. However, most of the examples we have seen until now had a parent component which grouped other routes as its child routes and displayed them within its own router outlet.

Let us say we have some configuration as shown in the following code and we want to group the routes:

```
const routes: Routes = [
  {path: 'home', component: HomeComponent},
  {path: 'next', component: NextComponent},
  {path: 'third', component: ThirdComponent},
  {path: 'login', component: LoginComponent},
  {path: '', redirectTo: 'home', pathMatch: 'full'},
  {path: '**', component: NotFoundComponent}
];
```

Let us see how this scenario looks diagrammatically:

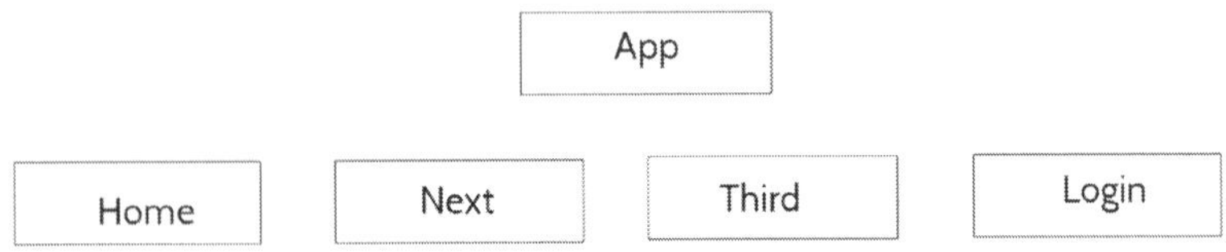

Fig 9.1

To group these routes, we can put them inside the children property of any one of these routes and contain them inside the router outlet of that parent route.

Let us take a look at the following code after grouping the routes:

```
const routes: Routes = [
  {path: 'home', component: HomeComponent},
  {path: 'next', component: NextComponent, children: [
```

```
    {path: 'third', component: ThirdComponent},
    {path: 'login', component: LoginComponent}
  ]},
  {path: '', redirectTo: 'home', pathMatch: 'full'},
  {path: '**', component: NotFoundComponent}
];
```

In this code, we have basically arranged the routes and grouped them inside one of the routes for the sake of better organization.

Let us see how this scenario looks diagrammatically now:

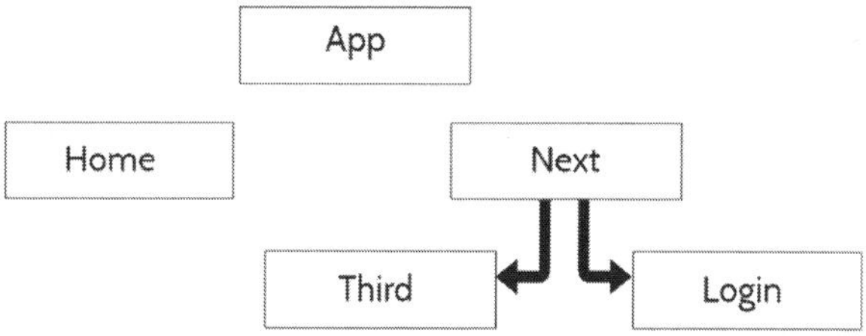

Fig 9.2

This is how we grouped our routes for better hierarchy and structure. However, if you now go and look at it in the browser, the routes that are grouped under the NextComponent do not work anymore. Does anyone want to take a guess at why does it happen?

That is when the concept of Component-less Routes comes in.

Component-less routes

The routes that do not have a component property in their configuration are not wrongly written but called **component-less routes**. Component-less routes are the ones which group the other routes for better structure but do not expect the router outlet to be placed within its router outlet. Why? Because there is no parent component now, so all the routes that have been grouped inside the component-less routes will all appear at a higher level and not within some other router outlet.

But where does the primary component go then? This component comes inside the grouping with the other grouped routes but with an empty path. Let us take a look at the following code and understand it better:

```
const routes: Routes = [
 {path: 'home', component: HomeComponent},
 {path: 'next', children: [
  {path: '', component: NextComponent},
  {path: 'third', component: ThirdComponent},
  {path: 'login', component: LoginComponent}
 ]},
 {path: '', redirectTo: 'home', pathMatch: 'full'},
 {path: '**', component: NotFoundComponent}
];
```

How is this code different from the previous code? Inside the children property, we have added another route with an empty path and the component to it. This component was previously put as a primary router outlet behaving as the parent component and expecting other routes to be displayed within its own router outlet.

Now all these three routes appear inside the grouped configuration and will be displayed at the same level without being inside any other route's router outlet.

How does this look diagrammatically now?

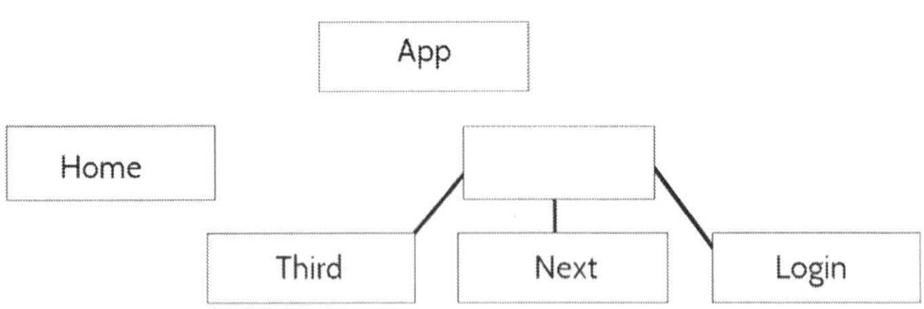

Fig 9.3

The preceding diagram very clearly explains the meaning of a component-less route which has many routes configured inside it.

When you go back to the browser now and check if these two routes work, you will notice that they work perfectly fine in their own router outlet view.

It is pretty clear by now why we need component-less routes but let us quickly look at it broadly now.

Why component-less routes?

As we saw, grouping definitely helps us to organize our routes in a better hierarchical structure. Also, in a large enterprise-level Angular application, where route configurations are huge, grouping them under component-less routes is a very safe idea.

The best part about grouping components under the component fewer routes is that you need not use the route guards and route resolvers for every child route separately. You can use the guard and resolvers with the component-less route and this will apply to all the route configurations that have been configured inside it.

Let us take a look at how this appears in the code:

```
const routes: Routes = [
  {path: 'home', component: HomeComponent},
  {path: 'next', canActivateChild: [CheckGuard], children: [
    {path: '', component: NextComponent},
    {path: 'third', component: ThirdComponent},
    {path: 'login', component: LoginComponent}
  ]},
  {path: '', redirectTo: 'home', pathMatch: 'full'},
  {path: '**', component: NotFoundComponent}
];
```

Now, this route guard will apply to all the configured routes inside the component-less route. Similarly, we can create a resolver and use it for all the routes configured inside the component-less route. We will see how Route resolvers work in the next chapter.

Not only this, by grouping routes for particular feature routes, we can also lazy load the configured routes for that feature route. Lazy loading is a very important concept of Angular routing and acts as one of the pillars of routing.

Summary

In this chapter, we covered the concept of grouping routes and creating component-less routes. We also saw how a component-less route groups every route inside it and uses common guards and route resolvers. In the next chapter, we will learn about route resolvers and how they make routing in Angular much more effective when dealing with any data.

CHAPTER 10

Route Resolvers

We have been coming across route resolvers for a long time now. In almost every topic, we discussed and saw the usage of route resolvers somewhere or the other. But you might be wondering why I put this topic a little later in the book. So, this chapter will sort of justify its placement here in the book.

We have seen different usages of routes now such as child routes loading the data within some template, secondary routes loading the routes as stand-alone at a higher level, route guards making the application much more effective by taking care of important things like security, monitoring, authorization, and so on. Now, in this chapter, we will see how the routes, as the name of this chapter clearly denotes, will get some data loaded before loading the whole template view. It might sound a little confusing now, but by the end of this chapter, you will be able to understand why this topic is known as **Resolving the routes**.

In this chapter, we will cover the following topics:

- What are route resolvers?
- Usage of route resolvers
- Adding route resolvers

What are route resolvers?

When we route from one view to another, and the template of the second view requires some data, we face a delayed loading of data in this view. The static data on the template loads as the user navigates to the route, whereas the data that is coming from the server through the APIs takes a long time to show up in the template view. This does not appear to be very responsive in an application. Partial loading of any view is not attractive at all. In such a case, we can load the data before actually routing the view so that when we receive all the data, i.e. static as well as the data that is to come from the server, then we can proceed to route to the next view with the full template ready.

By prefetching the data, we would not actually have to face the partial data loaded in the view. We can also reuse the data while prefetching and use the same code for the data access service. Prefetching also allows you to resolve any errors that we might have in the route before actually navigating to the next route.

Now there are different ways to get the data for your component view. This data can come from the angular-in-memory-web-api, or some service, or maybe from some local JSON file or you can also use the data property of the route configuration. This data property of the route configuration looks like this:

```
//Route Data Property
{
  path: 'user',
  component: UserComponent,
  data: {dataProp: 'UserData'}
}
```

In the code, route looks like this:

```
const routes: Routes = [

  {path: 'third', component: ThirdComponent, data:  {dataProp: 'UserData'}},
  {path: 'productedit', component: ProductEditComponent },
  {path: '', redirectTo: 'second', pathMatch: 'full'},

];

@NgModule({
  imports: [RouterModule.forRoot(routes)],
  exports: [RouterModule]
})
export class AppRoutingModule { }
```

Fig 10.1

And inside the component, refer to this data property as given in the following code:

```
this.dataProp = this.route.snapshot.data['dataProp'];
```

This is one way of getting the data; however, we can get the data from an Angular service to communicate among components that are not related to each other or via HTTP to create API calls to the server.

Before moving to the usages of route resolvers, let us understand how the process of resolving a route works. So, you route to a URL where you expect some data in the template. However, the static elements of that template appear in the view but the data coming from the backend loads in some time after the static data on the template. To solve this, resolvers actually prevent your view to be displayed before the data gets loaded. So, the component actually gets activated when your data has arrived at the view and the template can be displayed fully, not just with the static elements.

But how does it work?

So, with a route resolver, the data need not come to the component when it has been activated already. It comes to the resolver service which then gets ready with the data and activates the component to display the completely loaded template view. If we do not have a resolver, the click of a link/button will direct you to the view, load what is available, wait for the data to come from the server, and then display the rest of the data on the template.

Let us see how it looks diagrammatically (without the route resolver):

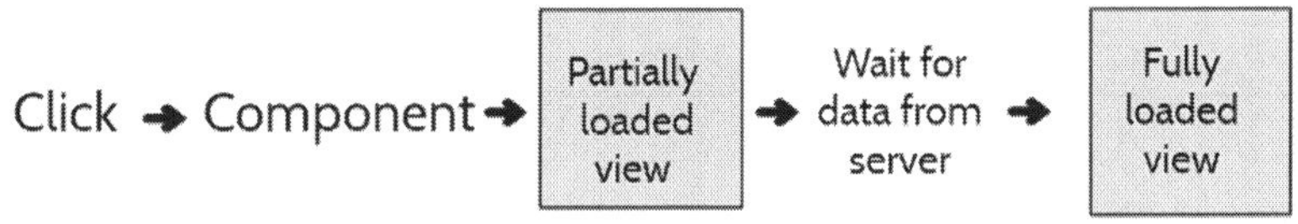

Fig 10.2

Without the route resolver, when you click on the link/button to navigate to the next route, the flow goes to the component template which is to be displayed. This then displays whatever data is available inside the template and then waits for the data from the server. In the meantime, the user gets a partially loaded view of the component's template. After it gets the data from the server, it shows up on the template and the view appears fully loaded.

Let us see how it looks diagrammatically (with the route resolver):

Fig 10.3

With the route resolver, however, the flow goes to the service instead of directly going to the component, and waits for the data from the server. Once it gets the complete data, it activates the component and displays the fully loaded component template view.

Uses of route resolvers

Working with route resolvers includes three steps in the process. Resolvers are created as Angular services so the first step is to build a custom Angular service for the data needed for our component. Once the service is created, we add the resolve property to the route configuration and use it to add the resolver to access the data for that particular route. After the route gets the data, which we need for the component, the component then reads the data from the activated route service.

In the previous chapter, we saw how to read the data from the `ActivatedRoute` service. It can be done using a snapshot or an observable. In case the data does not change and always remains the same, we use the snapshot. However, if the data that comes is expected to change, it is advisable to use an observable. Now let us read the following code:

```
//Building a Route Resolver Service
import { Injectable } from '@angular/core';
import { Resolve, ActivatedRouteSnapshot, RouterStateSnapshot } from '@angular/
router';
import { Observable } from 'rxjs';
import {User} from './user-data';
@Injectable({
  providedIn: 'root'
})
export class UserResolver implements Resolve<User> {
  resolve(route: ActivatedRouteSnapshot, state: RouterStateSnapshot):
Observable<User>{}
}
```

The ActivatedRouteSnapshot module gives us the information about the current route whereas the RouteStateSnapshot module tells about the state of the router. After calling the resolve method, the router calls in the data and then gets the component view loaded.

Inside the code, it looks as shown in the following screenshot:

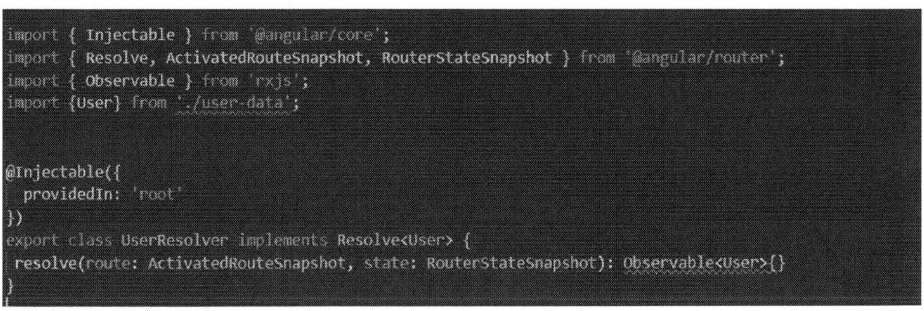

```
import { Injectable } from '@angular/core';
import { Resolve, ActivatedRouteSnapshot, RouterStateSnapshot } from '@angular/router';
import { Observable } from 'rxjs';
import {User} from './user-data';


@Injectable({
  providedIn: 'root'
})
export class UserResolver implements Resolve<User> {
 resolve(route: ActivatedRouteSnapshot, state: RouterStateSnapshot): Observable<User>{}
}
```

Fig 10.4

What does the resolve method do?

It calls the **get** method for the data and returns it to the component.

Use the resolve property inside the route configuration.

Adding the route resolvers

The following code snippet is an example of how to add the route resolvers:

```
{
 path: 'user',
 component: UserComponent,
 resolve: {user: UserResolver}
}
```

The resolver can be added as a key-value pair using the reference to the resolver service. Here in this example, we use the user as the key to reference to the UserResolver service:

```
const routes: Routes = [
  {path: 'second', canDeactivate: [GuardServicGuard], component: SecondComponent},
  {path: 'third', component: ThirdComponent, resolve: {user: UserResolver}},
  {path: 'productedit', component: ProductEditComponent },
  {path: '', redirectTo: 'second', pathMatch: 'full'},

];

@NgModule({
  imports: [RouterModule.forRoot(routes)],
  exports: [RouterModule]
})
export class AppRoutingModule { }
```

Fig 10.5

We can also use multiple resolver services for the component to ensure that the key for each of the resolver services is unique. Also, another important thing to ensure is to import the resolver service inside the module. You can refer to the following code:

```
import {UserResolver} from './user-resolver..service';
```

Reading the route resolvers

Now that we have created the resolver service and registered it inside the module as well, we are left with the last and the final step, that is, to read the data from the service. There is two ways of doing this, first by using a snapshot and second by using an observable. Let us first see when we do not have the changing data and it is static so that we can use a snapshot:

```
constructor(private route: ActivatedRoute){
  this.user = this.route.snapshot.data['user'];
}
```

Now that we have this non-changing data, we can get this inside the ngOnInit() lifecycle hook:

```
ngOnInit(){
  const <key>: UserResolver = this.route.snapshot.data['<key>'];
}
```

In our case, it should look like the following code:

```
ngOnInit(){
  const user: UserResolver = this.route.snapshot.data['user'];
}
```

We also need to pass this key and its value to the method that handles it, so inside the ngOnInit lifecycle hook, we use the following code:

```
ngOnInit(){
  const user: UserResolver = this.route.snapshot.data['user'];
  this.method(user.User)
}
```

If there is some data that changes every time it comes on the same page, we will use observables:

```
this.route.data.subscribe(data => {
  const user: User Resolver = data['user']
  this.method(user.User)
})
```

This gives a much better experience with changing data loading as and when the whole page loads and there is nothing like partial page loading. Also, if at runtime, an error occurs, resolvers will help you resolve the error before getting redirected to the next view. So, this becomes very helpful in error handling as well.

Summary

In the beginning of this chapter, resolvers sounded very vague in their usage. By the end of this chapter, we learned how resolvers help us in loading the pages fully without facing delayed responses in some of the data and also helps us perform error handling; for example, if an incorrect URL is passed. We also learned the ways of using the resolver service by using both the snapshot and observable.

In the next chapter, we will learn about the most used and talked about topic of Routing which is lazy loading your components and making routing in Angular much more effective.

CHAPTER 11

Lazy Loading

In this chapter, we dive deeper into the routing concepts and try to make our application much more effective by improving the performance and the starting the application, and how the components get loaded inside the application.

When the user starts his application, the request goes to the application server to load the required files. The time between the request sent by the user and the user actually receiving the data should be minimum. To do this, we use asynchronous routing which is also known as **lazy loading**.

In this chapter, we will learn the lazy loading of files and routes. In this chapter, we will cover the following topics:

- What is lazy loading?
- CanLoad guard
- Preloading strategy
- Custom strategy

What is lazy loading?

The first step to approach when working with lazy loading is looking at how Angular builds all the files that we require for the working for our application.

To do this, let us go inside our project and run npm start on the command line to see all the files it builds:

```
npm start
```

This is what the output of the command used will look like:

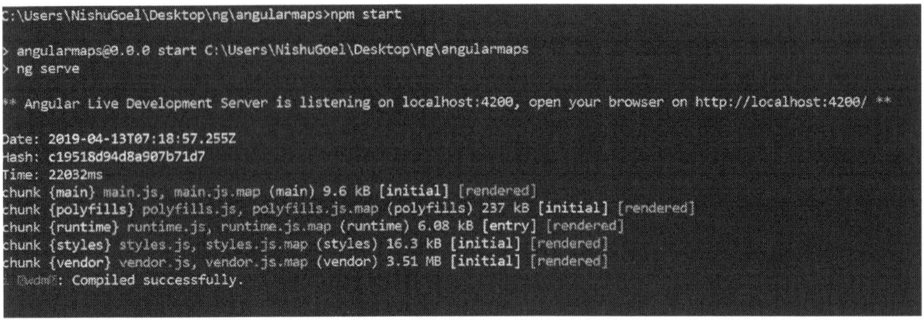

Fig 11.1

Now let us take a closer look at the files that have been built and try to understand what they are for.

The main.js file contains all the code in our application, the polyfills.js file loads all the polyfill scripts to make sure it can be compatible with all the modern browsers. The runtime.js loads all the other files. The styles.js file loads the styles as the name suggests and the vendor.js file loads all the imported libraries.

Also, let us take a look at the different sizes of these files which we will compare with the production generated files.

Now, let us run our application in the production mode using the following command:

ng serve -o –prod

Let us take a look at the following screenshot:

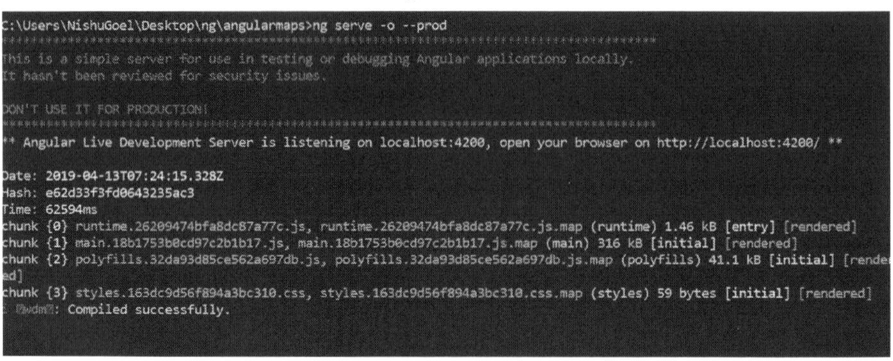

Fig 11.2

Look at the generated files now which are less in number and the size too is very small. Where did the vendor.js bundle go? So, the imported libraries are now inside the main.js bundle and the compilation process during the build does the **Ahead-of-Time** compilation (**AOT**) which loads the HTML and TypeScript code into JS files. This will render the application faster on the browser and the compiler does not need to be inside the bundle. The request would not need to load all the files from the server now which will improve the startup time of our application.

The main purpose of lazy loading is, therefore, to reduce the size of the only large-sized file now, which is main.js. We do this by lazy loading the files that are required occasionally. Its working is shown in the following screenshot:

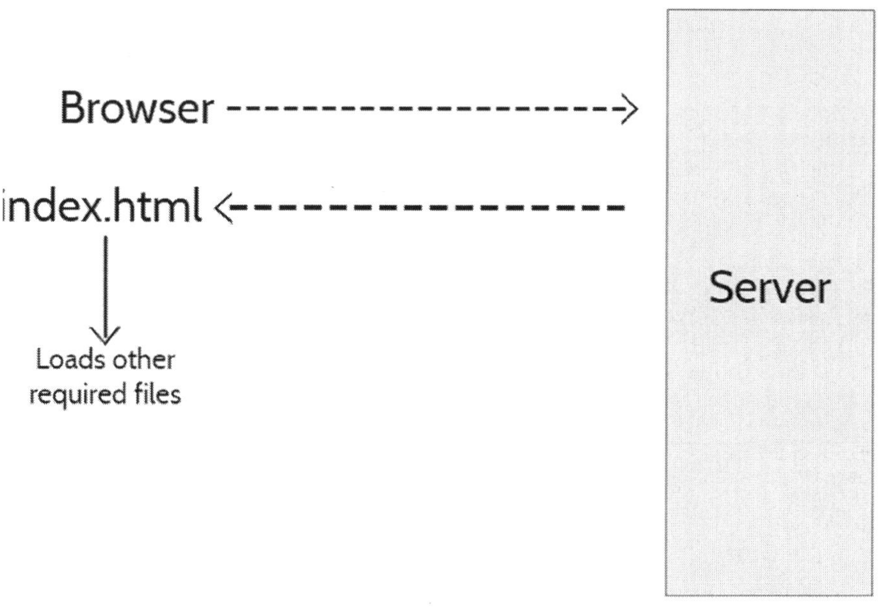

Fig 11.3

However, when lazy loading routes in Angular, the situation looks a bit different:

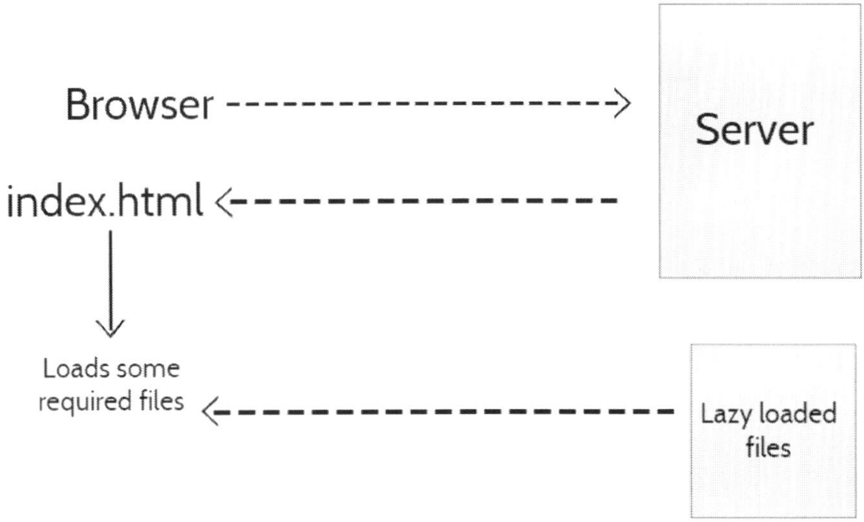

Fig 11.4

Whatever is the size of the applications; it does not make our application heavy and loads only what is required currently.

Working with lazy loading

Here are some of the important things to understand before working with a lazy loaded route:

- Lazy loading works on a feature module because it applies to a particular function of the application which should be defined inside its own specific module.
- Since lazy loading is configured on a parent route, we need to make sure that the routes are configured inside a parent route configuration as its children.
- The feature module should not be referenced in any other module because otherwise Angular will download the feature module also and compile it. This will definitely not solve our purpose of lazy loading the files.

To start lazy loading to asynchronously load the feature module for routing whenever required, we need to go to the route configuration and use the loadChildren property. Let us see what this property does:

```
{path: 'user', loadChildren: './users/user.module#UserModule'},
```

The loadChildren property is not something that is related to the children property that we saw in child routes. This property is only used for lazy loading the feature module.

Let us break down the property's values. The loadChildren property accepts a string value which contains the route to the feature module followed by a hash symbol and then the name of the feature module.

Now when the route gets activated, the loadChildren property will get activated and load the requested module. It will then load the requested component and display that component's template as shown in the following code:

// app-routing.module.ts

```
import { NgModule } from '@angular/core';
import { Routes, RouterModule } from '@angular/router';
import { HomeComponent } from './home/home.component';
import { NextComponent } from './next/next.component';
import { ThirdComponent } from './third/third.component';
import { NotFoundComponent } from './not-found/not-found.component';
import { LoginComponent } from './login/login.component';
import { CartComponent } from './cart/cart.component';
const routes: Routes = [
 {path: 'home', component: HomeComponent},
 {path: 'user', loadChildren: './user/user.module#UserModule'},
 {path: 'next',  children:[
  {path: '', component: NextComponent},
  {path: 'login', component: LoginComponent}
 ]},
 {path: 'third', component: ThirdComponent},
 { path: 'login', component: LoginComponent },
 { path: 'Cart', component: CartComponent },
```

```
 {path: '', redirectTo: 'home', pathMatch: 'full'},
 {path: '**', component: NotFoundComponent}
];
@NgModule({
 imports: [RouterModule.forRoot(routes)],
 exports: [RouterModule]
})
export class AppRoutingModule { }
```

Do not forget to remove the configuration of this route from the feature module. Once we have configured this property, we need to go to the console to see which files are generated.

We will see an extra bundle file generated.

Now, if you go the network tab in the console to see the files generated on routing to the UserModule module, you will see one extra file created with some numeric value which might look something like this:

Fig 11.5

This is how lazy loading gets implemented using the loadChildren feature in the route configuration for the specific feature module. This creates another bundle file only when that route is navigated to and the data is requested.

We now go to see the use of CanLoad guard in the lazy loading of routes.

We have seen how to use guards like canActivate, canDeactivate, etc. to authorize and monitor our application routes. However, when lazy loading the data, we can use the canLoad guard. Let us see how it works.

canLoad guard

So, the first thing about the canLoad guard is its meaning is clear from its name itself. This guard apparently tells to load a particular module only if it can be loaded. This means that we need to check the criteria before loading the module; otherwise, there is no need to even load this module if the requirements are not met. This secures our application from the users who do not have the access to view a particular component template.

So if we do not want the module to be loaded, we use canLoad guard, authorize the user, if successful, and then move to load the module. Let us take a look at the diagrammatic representation of the scenario we just discussed:

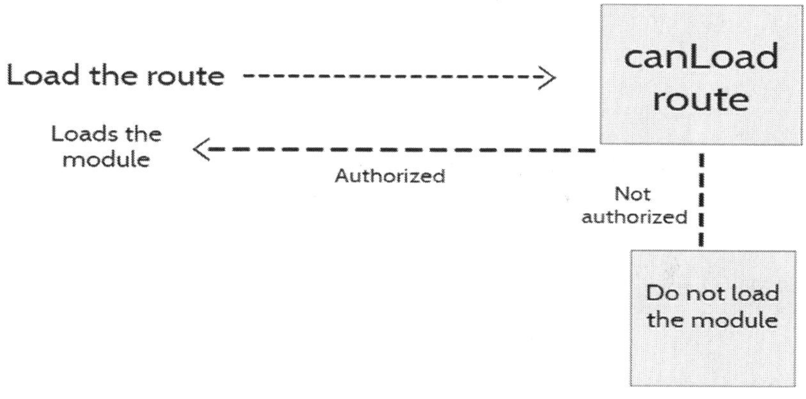

Fig 11.6

To create this guard, as we have seen earlier, we will import it inside a service:

```
import {CanLoad} from '@angular/router';
```

This canLoad guard also has a route property:

```
canLoad(route: Route): boolean {
  return this.method(route.path);
}
```

Put this guard inside the route configuration now:

```
{ path: 'user',
 canLoad: [AuthGuard],
 loadChildren: './user/user.module#UserModule'}
}
```

Now, after loading the page, it redirects you to the guard and if you see the files loaded inside the network tab of the console, you will notice that the module has not been loaded as yet. It will load only once the authorization of the user is complete. This scenario will appear like this:

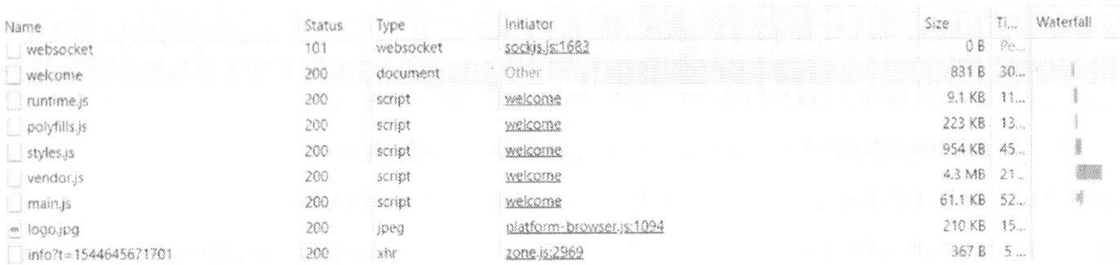

Fig 11.7

Now, if we cancel the authorization, the file will not need to load, and if the authorization is complete, then it will load the bundle file.

PreLoading modules

So, we have seen that when the user navigates from the root component template to the feature module, it has this waiting time to load this bundle file for this specific feature module and then the feature module template appears. However, when we are making everything perform efficiently, why not this?

So, instead of waiting for the router to load the feature module after the user requests for it, we can actually preload the data required in the backend and serve it as and when the user requests for it. This is what preloading means. Preloading is useful for loading those modules for which we know that at some point in time, we would definitely need to load the data for this module, and it is not based on the authorization of the user to access it or not.

This is also known as **eager lazy loading** and the name now describes why it is called so by itself.

To preload the data, the router provides us with the following three preloading techniques:

- No preloading: This is something we have been using by default because we were not pre-loading the data at all and loading it only after the user requests for it.
- Full pre-loading: In full pre-loading, we load all the lazy loaded modules before hand and serve them whenever they are requested for without having the waiting time.

To use full preloading, we use the preload key-value pair as the second argument to the forRoot/forChild array:

```
{preloadingStrategy: PreloadAllModules}
```

In the code, it looks like this:

```
RouterModule.forRoot([
 {path: 'home', component: HomeComponent},
 {path: 'user', loadChildren: './user/user.module#UserModule'},
 {path: 'next', children:[
  {path: '', component: NextComponent},
  {path: 'login', component: LoginComponent}
 ]},
 {path: 'third', component: ThirdComponent},
 { path: 'login', component: LoginComponent },
 { path: 'Cart', component: CartComponent },
 {path: '', redirectTo: 'home', pathMatch: 'full'},
 {path: '**', component: NotFoundComponent}
], {preloadingStrategy: PreloadAllModules})
```

This is how the scenario of preloading all the lazy loaded modules looks like:

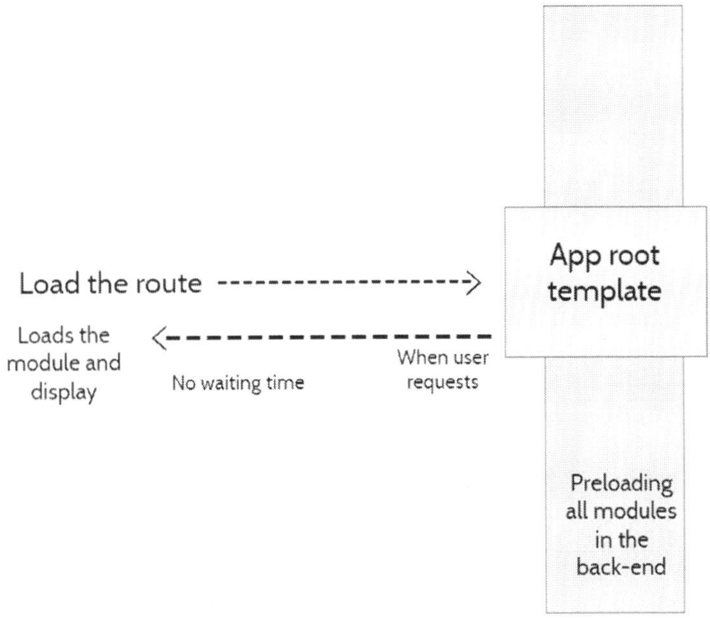

Fig 11.8

The two things we need to make sure of while implementing preloading are as follows:

Import `PreloadAllModules` inside Angular or the router.

Also, remember that the `canLoad` guards always blocks preloading, so if the `canLoad` guard is executed, preloading will not work. However, if we want preloading to work but at the same time, we want to secure access of the users to the route, we can replace the `canLoad` guard with the `canActivate` guard, and then it works perfectly fine.

Custom preloading modules

When we want to preload only some of the lazy loaded modules, we use custom preloading. We can preload some of the most commonly used lazy loaded modules but do not preload some other lazy loaded modules at all.

Building a custom preload strategy works similar to a guard. We create a service and set the preloading strategy routing option inside it.

To build this service, use the following code:

```
import { Injectable } from '@angular/core';
import {PreloadingStrategy} from '@angular/router';
import {Observable} from '@angular/router';
@Injectable({
  providedIn: 'root'
})
export class CustomStrategy implements PreloadingStrategy{
   preload(route: Route, load: Function): Observable<any>{
  }
}
```

The route property references to the route to be navigated to and the load function loads the custom preloading strategy. The preload method then finally implements the logic as to when to preload the lazy loaded modules.

Then, it is set as the second parameter to the route configuration:

```
{preloadingStrategy: CustomStrategy}
```

To define the load function, we can use the data property of the route configurations that we discussed in the previous chapters. Let us take a look at the following code:

```
preload(route: Route, load: Function): Observable<any>{
  if(route.data && route.data['preload']){
    return load();
  }
  return of(null);
}
```

Also, make sure that you define this data property in the route configuration as true:

```
{path: 'user',
 canActivate [AuthGuard],
 data: {preload: true},
 loadChildren: './user/user.module#UserModule'},
```

With the data property configured, the lazy loaded module will work as per the function load and load only the required lazy loaded modules as per the custom strategy service.

Summary

Using lazy loading to load modules improves the startup performance of our Angular application by loading only the required modules, and then when the user requests for a specific module, we will load it to provide the template for that. We also saw how we can preload the lazy loaded modules to avoid the waiting time and the three different strategies of preloading. We then saw how to preload all the lazy loaded modules or preload only some of them, whereas loading others only if and when required.

In the next chapter, we will deal with loads of data and perform different create, read, update, and delete operations on this data using routing.

CHAPTER 12

CRUD Operations with Routing

After having learnt almost all the concepts of routing, let us jump into dealing with data when performing Angular routing. In this chapter, we will see how to perform various operations on data with routing in an Angular application. The most required operations in almost any application that we work with are creating, reading, updating, and deleting the data which is what is known as CRUD operations. Now perform these operations on different routes bring in routing in the concept of CRUD operations.

By the end of this chapter, you will be able to understand how to deal with the data and these operations on different routes using all the concepts that you have learnt like route guards, loading data in a child route, using the auxiliary route to load the data, and more.

We will cover the following topics in this chapter:

- What are CRUD operations?
- Using in-memory-web-api
- Read data
- Create data
- Update data
- Delete data

What are CRUD operations?

Let us first take a look at CRUD operations.

The operations to be performed on the data are create, read, update, and delete which are collectively called CRUD operations. These operations are a must to perform when dealing with data that might be residing on the server or in a local file or anywhere else as shown in the following screenshot:

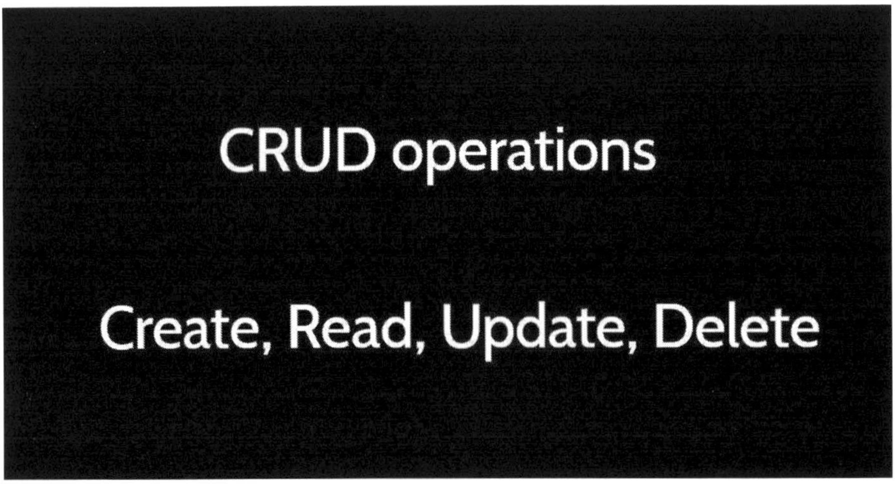

Fig 12.1

To get the data to perform these operations, we can send an HTTP request to the server, receive the data, and perform the operations. However, for testing and development purposes, we can use the angular-in-memory-web-api provided by the Angular official documentation. This angular-in-memory-web-api mocks the call to the backend server and gets the data for us to perform these operations on it. This angular-in-memory-web-api, however, is not a part of Angular core. When we say it mocks the call to the backend, it means that it will send the HTTP request to the local in-memory-data-store and get the data for us, thus making the task of dealing with data a lot easier. We can simply replace this service when working with the real server in a real-time application.

There are many other ways of faking the backend server to get the data such as creating a file with the hard coded data in it, using a local JSON file, and as discussed, using the angular-in-memory-web-api.

Using in-memory-web-api

To start, the very first task is to install angular-in-memory-web-api using the following command:

npm install angular-in-memory-web-api — save-dev

The save dev flag is used here to save this dependency that you will use for the development purpose.

Once done, you will be able to see it in the dependencies inside your package.json file as shown in the following screenshot:

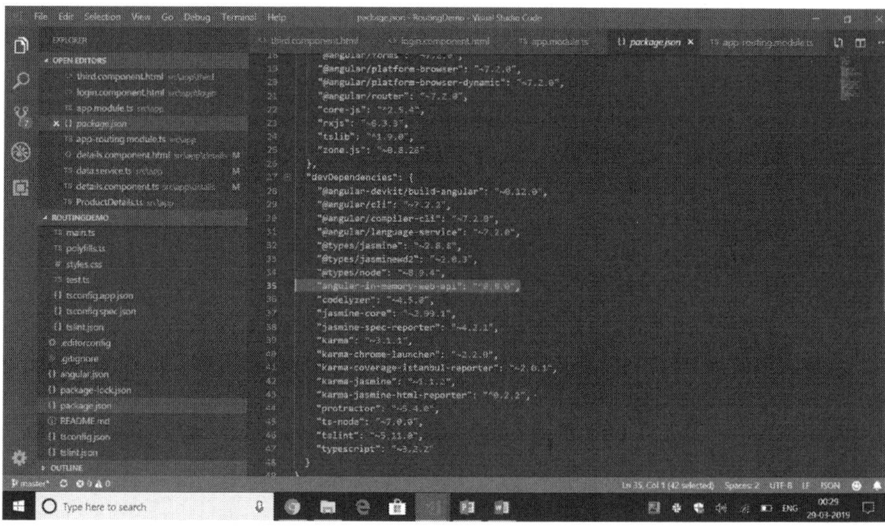

Fig 12.2

Now that we have this dependency saved in our application, we can go forward with using the angular-in-memory-web-api for performing CRUD operations inside our application.

Step one is to create an entity class where we mention the class name and its properties as shown in the following screenshot:

Fig 12.3

After our entity class is ready, we will implement InMemoryDbService inside a new class as a service. Let us take a look at the following code for this:

```
import {InMemoryDbService} from 'angular-in-memory-web-api';
import {User} from './user-data';
export class UserData implements InMemoryDbService {
 createDb(){
  const users: User[]=[
   { id: 1, name: 'Ram', email: 'ram@gmail.com', contact: '0000000000' },
   { id: 2, name: 'Shyam', email: 'sh@gmail.com', contact: '1111111111' },
   { id: 3, name: 'Mohan', email: 'moh@live.in', contact: '2222222222' },
   { id: 4, name: 'Rohan', email: 'rohan@gmail.com', contact: '6666666666' },
   { id: 5, name: 'Sumit', email: 'sumit@live.in', contact: '9909999999' }
  ];
  return {users};
 }
}
```

In the preceding code, we are overriding the createDb() method and creating a collection of the entity users which returns its collection in the end. The other thing that we do here is to import the InMemoryDbService module. To use all these, we need to register these inside the module as shown in the following screenshot:

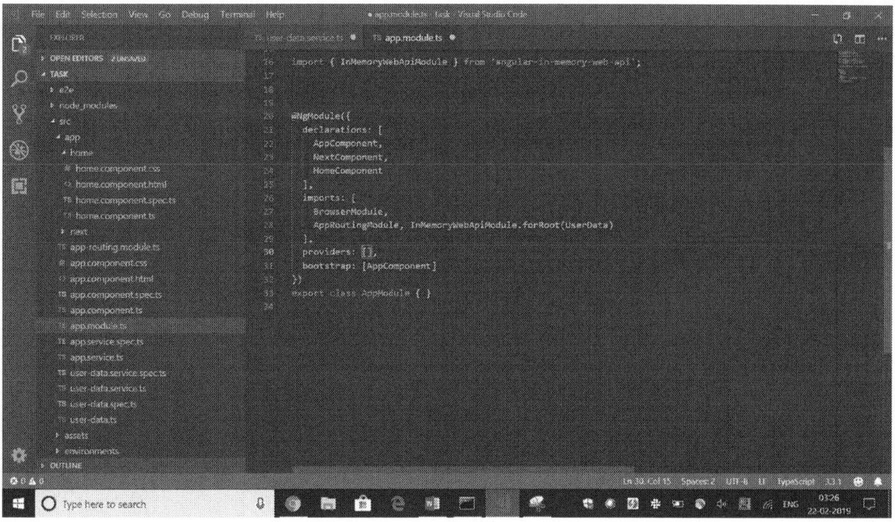

Fig 12.4

After we have registered it inside the module, we are finally ready to perform the CRUD operations using the angular in-memory web API now.

To do this, let us create a service and perform HTTP operations inside that as shown in the following code snippet:

```
import { Injectable } from '@angular/core';
import {HttpClient, HttpHeaders} from '@angular/common/http';
import {Observable, throwError} from 'rxjs';
import { tap, catchError } from 'rxjs/operators';
import {User} from './user-data';
@Injectable({
  providedIn: 'root'
})
export class DataService {
  apiurl = 'api/users';    // Our created Data can be accessed here at api/users
    headers = new HttpHeaders().set('Content-Type', 'application/json').set('Accept',
'application/json');
  httpOptions= {
    headers: this.headers
```

```
  };
constructor(private http: HttpClient) { }  //Injecting HTTP service communicate with
the data  private handleError(error: any) {
    console.error(error); //Created a function to handle and log errors, in case
    return throwError(error);
  }
}
```

Now, let us try to understand this code. We have created the service DataService. Inside this service, we access the data through the remote API with the help of this line of code:

```
apiurl = 'api/users';
```

The next step is to inject the HttpClient service but before we do this, we need to import some important files:

```
import {HttpClient, HttpHeaders} from '@angular/common/http';
import {Observable, throwError} from 'rxjs';
import { tap, catchError } from 'rxjs/operators';
```

In the preceding code, we are setting the httpOptions variable to perform HTTP operations. Now, finally we need to read the data which we receive through this remote call.

Read data

To read the data from the API, we need to use the http.get() method inside the service that we just created.

We will read the data with the help of observables returned from the newly created User array as shown in the following code snippet:

```
getUsers(): Observable<User[]> {
    return this.http.get<User[]>(this.apiurl).pipe(
      tap(data => console.log(data)),
      catchError(this.handleError)
    );
  }
}
```

Now, we need to read this data on a routed component and not on the home component.

To do this, we use DataService inside the component where you want this data to appear. So, let us say you have a home component which routes to different component views from reading, creating, and deleting data. It looks something like this:

Fig 12.5

To read the data now, you need to use the getUsers method inside another component which will be routed to when the user clicks on **Get Users**.

Inside the GetUsers component, use the following code:

```
users: User[] = [];
 constructor(private dataservice: DataService){}
 getUsers(){
  this.dataservice.getUsers().subscribe(data => {
   this.users = data;
  });
 }
```

We call the getUsers() method and return the data to the created variable users. We also call the getUsers() method inside the ngOnInit() life cycle hook.

In the template of the GetUserComponent object, use the data to be displayed. You can refer to the following code:

```
<div align='center'><h1>List of Users</h1></div>
<table class ="table table-striped" >
 <tr *ngFor="let u of users">
  <td>
```

```
    {{u.id}}
   </td>
   <td>
    {{u.name}}
   </td>
   <td>
    {{u.model}}
   </td>
  </tr>
</table>
```

This is how it appears on the browser after fetching the list of users:

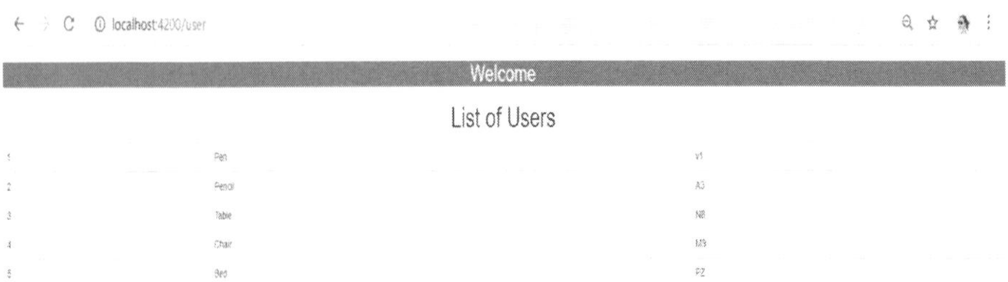

Fig 12.6

Reading the data from the server is the easiest of all CRUD operations and performing the read of data is not very similar to how the functionality for creating, updating and deleting the data would work. We need to fetch the user with a particular ID to update or delete that particular user. Similarly, to create a new user as the data, we would need the details to be input and then need to save them as some initialized `User` array.

Fetch data

To perform this, let us first see how to get a user with a particular ID:

```
getUser (id: number): Observable<UserFetch> {
 const url = `${this.apiurl}/${id}`;
 return this.http.get<UserFetch>(url).pipe(
  catchError(this.handleError)
 );
```

```
}
```

The following code snippet is from the component.ts file:

```
fetchId = 1;
getUser() {
  this.dataservice.getUser(this.fetchId).subscribe(data => {
    this.user = data;
   this.displayData= true;
  });
}
```

We can then create an input box on the template asking the user to input the id of users they want to fetch the details of and then display the fetched user details. This would look like as shown in the following screenshot:

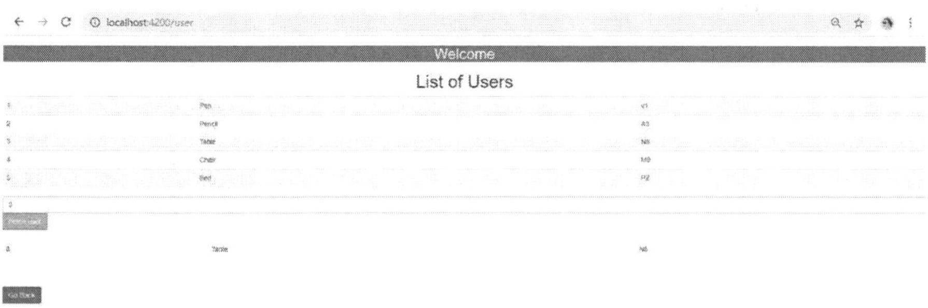

Fig 12.7

Create data

To create the data in the API, we need to perform the HTTP POST operation and pass the data that needs to be inserted in the database.

We will use the addUser() method for this. Since we want to create the user on a different route now, we will use this method to add the user on the CreateUserComponent object.

Inside the data service, add the following code:

```
addUser (user: UserFetch): Observable<UserFetch> {
 user.id=null;
```

```
 return this.http.post<UserFetch>(this.apiurl, user, this.httpOptions).pipe(
  tap(data => console.log(data)),
  catchError(this.handleError)
 );
}
```

On the CreateUser component, use the addUser method:

```
export class CreateUserComponent implements OnInit {
 userFormGroup: FormGroup;
 users: User[];
 user: UserFetch;

 constructor(private dataservice: DataService){}
 getUsers(){
  this.dataservice.getUsers().subscribe(data => {
   this.users = data;
  });
 }
 ngOnInit() {
  this.userFormGroup = new FormGroup(
   {
    name : new FormControl(''),
    model : new FormControl('')
   },
  );
  this.getUsers();
}
addUser() {
 this.dataservice.addUser(this.userFormGroup.value).subscribe(data => {
  this.user = data;
  console.log(this.user);
 });
 this.getUsers();
}}
```

The output will look like this:

Fig 12.8

After adding the user, it adds it to the `User` list:

Fig 12.9

Update data

Similarly, now to update the data, we will take the id of the user we want to update and update the age of that particular user. We can perform this in the `GetUser` template view itself, as we do not need to route to a new view to update the user on the component.

To do this, let us add it to the service first:

```
updateUser(user: UserFetch): Observable<UserFetch>{
  const url = `${this.apiurl}/${user.id}`;
  return this.http.put<UserFetch>(this.apiurl, user, this.httpOptions).pipe(
   map(() => user),
    catchError(this.handleError)
  );
}
```

An important thing to notice here is that whenever we need to perform the update operation, we use the http.put() method.

On the component.ts file, use the following code snippet:

```
idtoUpdate = 0;
 updateUser() {
  this.dataservice.getUser(this.idtoUpdate).subscribe(data => {
   this.user = data;
   this.user.model = 'Updated Model';
   this.dataservice.updateUser(this.user).subscribe(data1 => {
    this.getUsers();
   });
  });
 }
```

On the browser, enter the id to update the user with any value. We have currently taken the value as **Updated Model Value**. However, we can take the value as an input from the user too:

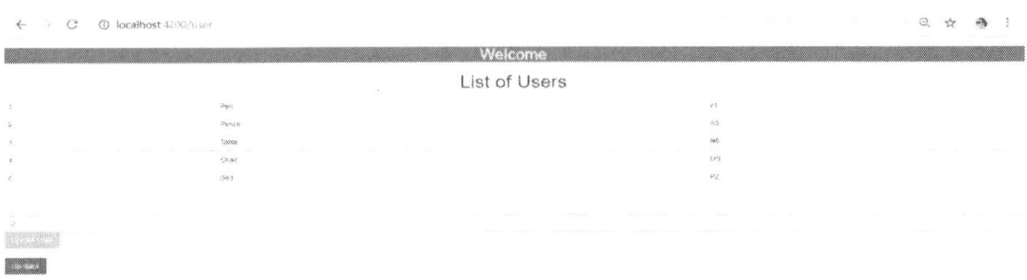

Fig 12.10

The default value of the id to update is taken to be zero and then when the user puts in the id to be updated, it fetches the user associated with that particular id and updates the value required to be updated:

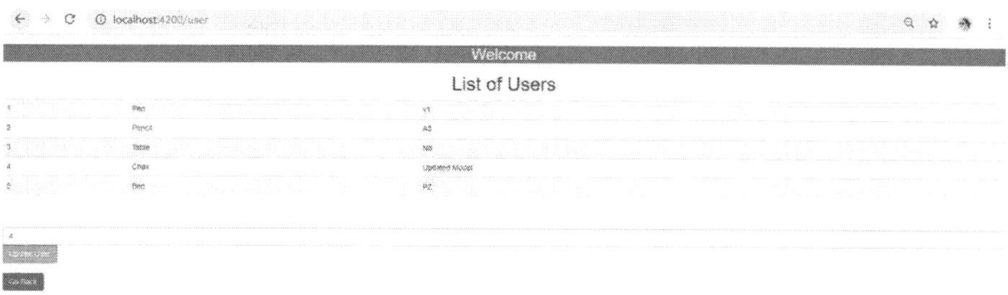

Fig 12.11

This updates the value of the particular user. Now, coming to the deletion of data from a different route.

Delete data

To delete the data from the list of users, add the delete operation to the service as shown in the following code:

```
deleteUser(id: number): Observable<UserFetch> {
const url = `${this.apiurl}/${id}`;
 return this.http.delete<UserFetch>(url, this.httpOptions).pipe(
   catchError(this.handleError)
 );
}
```

On the DeleteUserComponent, we subscribe to the observable using the following code:

```
idtodelete=0;
 deleteUser() {
  this.dataservice.deleteUser(this.idtodelete).subscribe(data => {
   this.getUsers();
  });
 }
```

We will get the following screenshots as output:

Fig 12.12

This is screenshot of the window after deletion is performed:

Fig 12.13

This deletes the user of the entered id from the **Delete User** route.

And this is how using routing, we can implement the CRUD operations with the angular-in-memory-web-api service.

Summary

In this chapter, we discussed how to create an in-memory data store to mock the call to the API and generate a service to get the data from this API. We performed the http.get() method to read data, the http.post() method to create data, the http.put() method to update data, and the http.delete() method to delete data by routing to different component templates.

You should now be able to:

- Create routes in Angular.
- Navigate to the different routes.
- Use multiple router outlets in the same view using named router outlets.

- Work with child routes and secondary routes.
- Load routes with routes using the child route configurations.
- Understand the usage of route guards and route resolvers to make your application more effective.
- Use asynchronous routing, that is, lazy loading modules to improve the startup performance of your application.
- Understand why grouping the routes under component-less routes helps.
- Understand why it is always better to organize your routes and modules into a better hierarchy using feature modules.
- Understand why feature modules are needed to perform lazy loading.
- Preload data with the techniques to preload all modules, and you will be able to also preload only the required lazy loaded modules using the custom preloading strategy.

Remember how `canLoad` guard blocks preloading but this can be fixed by replacing the `canLoad` guard with `canActivate` guard.

Printed in Great Britain
by Amazon

34981568R00077